The Purpose of Life

A theistic perspective

Stewart Goetz

continuum

Continuum International Publishing Group
A Bloomsbury company

50 Bedford Square	80 Maiden Lane
London	New York
WC1B 3DP	NY 10038

www.continuumbooks.com

© Stewart Goetz 2012

Library of Congress Cataloging-in-Publication Data
A catalog record for this book is available at the Library of Congress.

ISBN: HB: 978-1-4411-9035-2
PB: 978-1-4411-8082-7

Typeset by Deanta Global Publishing Services, Chennai, India

Bingham
people aren't
not taking
care of themselves
+ then saying it's
you right?

The Purpose of Life

For Kathryn and Andrew
Two of the three greatest sources
of happiness in my life

"Philosophy is perfectly right in saying that
life must be understood backwards. But then
one forgets the other clause—that it must be
lived forwards."

(Kierkegaard 1967, 450)

CONTENTS

PREFACE

For the past several years, I have regularly taught a class that I simply entitle "The Meaning of Life." I am not sure what students expect when they enroll in the course, though one expressed to me after receiving a less-than-average grade on an exam that "I thought this would be a course where we could just bullshit about life." The class surely isn't that. Instead, it is an exploration of a wide variety of perspectives written by very thoughtful people about a topic that is at the heart of any serious consideration about what it is to be human.

In preparation for teaching "The Meaning of Life," I have read many papers and books about life's meaning that have been authored in recent years. The growing body of literature reflects a resuscitation of interest in the topic after decades in which it was not taken very seriously. The lack of professional philosophical interest in the meaning of life was part and parcel of a logical positivist philosophical movement in the first half of the twentieth century that dismissed as meaningless gibberish any statement that was not empirically verifiable (roughly, the idea was that a statement about the meaning of life is akin to "twas brillig, and the slithy toves did gyre and gimble in the wabe," because one cannot know it to be true or false through the use of one or more of one's five senses—even with the aid of scientific instruments). However, with the demise of logical positivism, which for the most part was a result of people coming to their senses and asking whether the proposition "No statement that is not empirically verifiable is meaningful" is itself empirically verifiable, philosophers once again began to engage a topic that nonphilosophers or lay persons never ceased to regard as both meaningful and important. But while the meaning of life is once again a legitimate philosophical topic for discussion among those in the academy, treatments of the issue have for the most part come from the pens of atheists and agnostics. There have been very few investigations of the topic written from a theistic perspective (the perspective of one who believes that God exists) that state what the meaning of life is and address the best arguments of atheists and agnostics. Hence, when I was approached by Haaris Naqvi of Continuum Press to write this book, I gladly accepted the challenge. It will, I believe, fill a gap in the contemporary literature on the meaning of life.

Though this book is written from a theistic and, therefore, religious perspective, it is a thoroughly reasoned treatment of the meaning of life that makes no appeal to "faith." This will strike some as odd, if not impossible. For example, Anthony Kronman, in his intriguing book *Education's End: Why Our Colleges and Universities Have Given Up on the Meaning of Life*, writes that

> every religion at some point demands a "sacrifice of the intellect." This point may come sooner or later, but every religion eventually reaches it. Every religion insists that at some point thinking is no longer adequate to the question of life's meaning, and that further progress can be made only by means other than thought. All religions recognize the finitude of human reason .... [E]very religion also affirms the existence and spiritual value of some attitude other than thought that has the power to carry us beyond the limits of reason if we are prepared to adopt it. And all declare that the deeper peace and greatest insight come when we take this step beyond reason's frontiers and open ourselves to the wisdom that "surpasseth understanding." (Kronman 2007, 198–9)

Contrary to what Kronman states, I, as a religious person, believe that it is not necessary to go beyond the bounds of reason when thinking long and hard about life's meaning. While I readily recognize the limitations of human reason, I believe that deep insight into the meaning of life lies within its bounds.

Like some other recent books about life's meaning (Julian Baggini's *What's It All About?* immediately comes to mind), I have written *The Purpose of Life: A Theistic Perspective* for a broadly educated reader who does not necessarily have a background in philosophy. I have worked hard to keep technical terminology to a minimum. In those places where I could not see any way to avoid it without sacrificing accuracy, I have labored to explain things as clearly as I can. Of course, the reader will be the ultimate judge about how well I have succeeded.

Throughout the following chapters, I interact extensively with the work of other authors. However, a reader will probably notice that I favorably quote one author more than any other. This author is C. S. Lewis. Though Lewis is probably not read by many professional philosophers these days (at least, his work is seldom cited), he was and remains someone whose thought deserves serious consideration. Hence, when I agree with him, which is often, I am happy to cite him as a kindred spirit.

While the book is entitled *The Purpose of Life: A Theistic Perspective*, I will for the most part discuss the theistic perspective in its Christian form. This is so for two major reasons. First, I am a practicing Christian and, therefore, am most familiar with the Christian theistic tradition. However, from what I know about other theistic traditions, such as Judaism and Islam, there is nothing that I say about God that either cannot be found in or is incompatible with one or more incarnations of those traditions. Second, I am an English-speaking analytical philosopher who for the most part reads the works of other English-speaking analytical philosophers. When they write about God's possible relevance to a meaningful life, they typically refer to Christian literature about God. Hence, my discussion of their work once again situates me in the Christian theistic tradition.

I make no apology for this Christian lens on the meaning of life but simply alert the reader to its reality. As Baggini points out, we hear much today about keeping an open mind, which many individuals take to imply that a commitment to any view is narrow-minded and chauvinistic. Baggini claims that this position is both vacuous and impossible to adhere to, and I agree. It is vacuous because "[o]ne cannot remain equally open to all possibilities or else one ends up believing nothing" (Baggini 2004, 152). It is impossible because "[e]ven to decide not to decide … is to make a decision that one way of life—that of suspension of belief—is better than the alternatives" (Baggini 2004, 152). Baggini rightly goes on to say that each of us has a hierarchy of beliefs, some more fundamental than others (Baggini 2004, 153–6). Given limitations of time and place, none of us is able to examine every claim that is incompatible with one's more basic beliefs. For example, as a Christian theist I simply do not have the time to investigate every other form of theism under the sun to see if it is superior to Christianity, just as Baggini, who as an atheist materialist denies the existence of the soul, does not have the time to examine every claim that might support the existence of the soul. Rather, what each of us does is carefully consider what we regard as the strongest challenges to our most basic convictions and let the chips fall where they may. In Baggini's own words, "you do your long and hard thinking at the most general level possible and don't bother to examine every specific example of the kind of belief you have dismissed.... We narrow our minds not just to avoid wasting mental energy but because we have to" (Baggini 2004, 153, 155).

Because I am defending a theistic view of the meaning of life, I make frequent reference to God, and given what I have just stated about my treatment of the topic from a Christian perspective, it should come as no surprise that when it is necessary to employ a pronoun to refer to God I use either "He," "His," or "Him." I have my reasons for doing so and fully recognize that my usage will please some and disturb others. There is no "win-win" approach I can take that will satisfy everyone. However, two points are relevant. First, I in no way believe that God is male, just as I in no way believe that God is female. Within most major theistic traditions, God is believed to be a bodiless being, a soul or spirit if you will, and I too affirm the same. While it is true that within the Christian version of theism God became embodied or incarnate in Jesus of Nazareth, God the Father always was and remains a disembodied being. Second, no philosophical point that I make in this book depends in the least on whether I refer to God as "He," "She," or "It." So, the reader should not lose the forest for a tree.

Most of the material that follows in subsequent chapters is theoretical in nature. This means that I will not be offering the reader much practical advice about how to lead his or her life. For reasons that will become evident in subsequent chapters, what practical advice I do give will extend no further than the admonition that one should obey one's conscience for the purpose of doing what one believes is right, when one's conscience informs one that one should act in a certain way. Because conscience is concerned with what is good, it is inviolable. So having forewarned the reader about the limited nature of my practical advice, I press ahead with the theoretical with the hope that it will justify the practical.

ACKNOWLEDGMENTS

I owe a great debt of gratitude to the students who have enrolled in and endured my meaning of life courses over the years. They have helped me to sharpen my thoughts on the topic at hand. I also owe thanks to Del Lewis, J. P. Moreland, Nate Simasek, and Charles Taliaferro, each of whom read the manuscript in its entirety and commented on it. I am especially indebted to my son, Andrew Goetz, for reading several drafts of the manuscript, talking over numerous points with me, and making so many valuable suggestions. A graduate student in mathematics, Andrew used his keen mind to help me clarify my thoughts on many issues. The former academic dean of Ursinus College, Judith Levy, deservedly has my deepest gratitude for supporting my request for a sabbatical leave in which I had the time to devote full attention to writing this book. A grant provided by the John Templeton Foundation enabled me to buy additional course release time and I thankfully acknowledge the Foundation for its financial support. I am also grateful to Subitha Nair for her assistance with the final preparations of the manuscript. Finally, I thank the love of my life, my wife Carolyn, for listening to me chatter on over the years about the topic of this book. I doubt that the book would ever have been written without her constant support.

1
Clarifying the question

What is the meaning of life?

Several years ago, many of my relatives gathered to celebrate my parents' 50th wedding anniversary. Present at the celebration were some aunts, uncles, and cousins whom I had not seen in 25 or 30 years. I chatted at varying lengths with most of them, but one conversation with a cousin was especially intriguing. After we had exchanged pleasantries and inquired about each other's families, we turned to discussing our jobs. "So what's your line of work, Stewart?" my cousin asked. "I'm a philosophy professor," I answered. Not many people know what to say in response to that answer, and my cousin didn't either. After staring at me briefly with a good bit of unease, he jokingly shot back "So, what's the meaning of life?" I smiled, and said "Well, you might be interested to know that there has actually been a good bit of agreement about the answer to that question down through the ages." "Really?" he responded. "Yes," I continued, "Many who have thought about the question have concluded that happiness is the meaning of life." I will never forget my cousin's reply: It was an extended "Hmmm."

In the fifth century, the Christian philosopher/theologian St Augustine wrote "For who wishes anything for any other reason than that he may become happy? ... It is the decided opinion of all who use their brains that all men desire to be happy" (Augustine 1993, IV. 23; X.1). Augustine's comment has always seemed to me to be eminently reasonable, and the overall aim of this book is to explain why it is plausible to hold that perfect happiness is the meaning of life. In saying that Augustine's answer has always seemed to me to be eminently reasonable, I mean literally that: it has seemed *reasonable* in the sense that it has seemed to me to be convincing in its own right, without any appeal to religion in the form of either a religious text or a special revelation from God to either a particular individual or a group. Thus, while the answer that I will give to the question "What is the meaning of life?" is a religious one, in the sense that it requires God's existence and creative activity, it will be a religious answer that is arrived at through the exercise of reason alone. In this sense, it can rightly be understood as the result of an exercise in what is broadly thought of as natural theology, which is traditionally taken to be the use of reason to argue for the existence of God. I say "broadly thought of as natural theology" because what I argue in this book is in no way meant to be an argument for the existence of God in the narrow sense of a rational demonstration from either incontrovertible or undeniably true premises. Rather, what I argue is that *if* we are to believe that life is ultimately meaningful or nonabsurd (and by "ultimately" I mean roughly "in the end, when all is said and done"), then we will be rationally driven to admit that God exists.

To begin my exercise in reason, I turn in the next section to explaining what I think is being asked when someone like my cousin queries "What is the meaning of life?" I summarize three different treatments of this question for the purpose of clarifying what I take to be its most plausible sense. In considering these three answers, I assume that a person who asks "What is the meaning of life?" is concerned about the meaning of *his or her own life*. Questions about the meaning of life in a broader sense (e.g. "What, if anything, is the meaning of the human race or the universe as a whole?"), if they are of interest to anyone, are not the subject matter of the question that interests me in this book.

Clarifying questions and answers to them

Consider the following three questions:

1 What is the meaning of life?
2 What makes life meaningful?
3 Is life meaningful?

While questions (1) through (3) are similar on their surfaces, they can reasonably be understood to be asking different things. Take (1). A plausible reading of it is "What is the purpose of life?" (2) can reasonably be read as asking "What makes life worth living?" And (3) naturally translates into something like "Does life make any sense in terms of things fitting together in an intelligible way?" Though questions (1) through (3) ask different things, they are interrelated in the sense that how one answers one of them goes a long way toward determining how one answers the other two. At least, that is what I will attempt to establish in what follows. To help answer these three questions, I turn to various philosophers' treatments of life's meaning.

In a fascinating discussion of the meaning of life, the philosopher Richard Taylor suggests that to answer the question "What is a meaningful life?" we should first focus on the question "What is a meaningless life?" (Taylor 2000, 167). To answer the latter question, Taylor has us consider a mythical story that was told by the ancient Greeks. According to this myth, a cruel king, Sisyphus, betrayed divine secrets to mortals. As punishment for his betrayal, he was condemned by the gods to roll a stone to the top of a hill, only to have it roll back down, and then once again to roll it to the top, only to have it roll back down again, *ad infinitum*. If ever there were a meaningless existence, this would seem to be it. Taylor suggests that the reason why Sisyphus' life seems meaningless is that Sisyphus never accomplishes anything. Hence, it immediately comes to mind that one way to introduce meaningfulness into Sisyphus's life is to have him get the stone to stay on the top of the hill. In the same vein of thought, it is possible to go a step further and suppose that Sisyphus not only gets the stone to remain on top of the hill, but he also incorporates it into a temple that he is building to the gods. According to Taylor, at a minimum, we learn from the story of Sisyphus that meaninglessness is endless futility in the attempt to accomplish a *purpose*, *goal*, or *end*. In contrast, meaningfulness involves not only the idea of a purpose or goal, but also the achievement, accomplishment, or satisfaction of it. Without the achievement of a purpose one is trying to accomplish, meaningfulness is only a hoped-for reality.

Taylor, however, is not done with the story of Sisyphus. He believes there is more that we can learn from it. Hence, he suggests that instead of altering the story by having Sisyphus get the stone to stay on top of the hill and, perhaps, incorporate it into a temple, we tweak it in a different way. This time, we keep Sisyphus continually rolling the stone to the top of the hill only to have it roll back down again, *ad infinitum*, but implant a *desire* in him to roll stones. Taylor admits that such a desire would be strange to us, but we can nevertheless suppose for the purpose of our trying to understand what it is that makes for a meaningful life that Sisyphus desires to roll stones. Given this desire, Taylor says that Sisyphus' life once again appears meaningful, because in this case he desires that he roll stones and satisfies or fulfills this desire (fulfilling a desire is achieving the desired purpose). Sisyphus' life is a meaningful one because he satisfies his preeminent desire in life. Taylor goes on to point out that rolling stones is an action or activity and that Sisyphus' life would be meaningful even if his action never results in the stone's remaining on top of the hill to be incorporated into a temple. The action itself could be the final purpose that is desired and whose accomplishment makes Sisyphus' life meaningful.

The myth of Sisyphus mentions the gods, but as far as Taylor is concerned, they are an essential ingredient of neither the story nor what we can learn from it about a meaningful life. The existentialist philosopher Jean-Paul Sartre believes otherwise (Sartre 1995). According to him, the existence of the gods or God is all important. To explain why, he asks us to consider an artifact (he suggests a paper-cutter, e.g. a pair of scissors) that is made by an artisan (a creator or designer). According to Sartre, the artifact exists and has a purpose because it originates with an idea in the mind of the artisan who makes it. In Sartre's well-known terminology, the artifact's essence (the content of the idea of the artifact that is in the artificer's mind) precedes its existence. Like Taylor, then, Sartre believes that what is at the heart of understanding the meaning of life is the notion of a purpose. Unlike Taylor, however, Sartre suggests that the idea of a purpose must be linked to the concept of a human person being an artifact. Thus, a human person can have a meaningful life only if his or her existence is the result of the creative activity of an artisan. Sartre believes that an artisan of this kind is what most people naturally have in mind when they think of God.

Finally, I turn to a thought-provoking treatment of the meaning of life by the philosopher Thomas Nagel (Nagel 2000). Nagel believes that to understand correctly what is at issue in thinking about the meaning of life, we must first be clear about a typical understanding of the concept of absurdity, which he illustrates with the following examples:

> In ordinary life a situation is absurd when it includes a conspicuous discrepancy between pretension or aspiration and reality: someone gives a complicated speech in support of a motion that has already been passed; a notorious criminal is made president of a major philanthropic foundation; you declare your love over the telephone to a recorded announcement; as you are being knighted, your pants fall down. (Nagel 2000, 178)

As Nagel goes on to point out, when one finds oneself in an absurd situation that involves a desire, one typically thinks about trying to change that situation by either changing the world so that it fulfills one's desire or changing (getting rid of) the desire itself. Similarly, if life is meaningless or absurd because of an unfulfilled desire, one is naturally inclined to think that one might eliminate meaninglessness and introduce meaningfulness either by getting rid of the desire or by changing the world so that it brings about the satisfaction of that desire. As Nagel sees things, however, what it is natural to think in this context is mistaken. The reason it is mistaken has to do with a peculiar quality of being human that ensures that one's life will be forever absurd. This peculiar quality is the capacity to "step back" and reflectively consider one's life and question it.

To explain what he has in mind, Nagel has us contrast the practice of justifying the various pursuits in our lives in terms of purposes with the reflective act of questioning the justifications themselves. For example, in life we justify taking aspirin by the purpose that it will eliminate a headache and justify preventing a child from touching a hot burner for the purpose of preventing bodily harm and pain. Absurdity in such contexts would arise if the action taken were not justified by the purpose, in which case there would be a discrepancy or mismatch. However, part of what makes us human is our self-consciousness and the ability to step back and ask higher-order questions from the outside, as it were, about the justifications of our pursuits in life. What we discover with this backward step is that our practice of providing justificatory purposes presupposes that we take those purposes seriously. We are taking those purposes seriously, "whether we are concerned primarily with fame, pleasure, virtue, luxury, triumph, beauty, justice, knowledge, salvation, or mere survival" (Nagel 2000, 178). Each of us lives his or her life with a serious regard for our purposes, even if the purpose were that we not take anything seriously. Now, in light of the distinctive capacity to step back and reflectively consider our lives with their pursuits and justifying purposes, each of us at some point inevitably asks "Why am I taking this purpose seriously? What *justifies* my doing so?" According to Nagel, it is at this higher level of questioning that a new form of inescapable philosophical absurdity is encountered. As has already been indicated, we judge a situation in life involving a pursuit and its explanatory purpose absurd when that pursuit and the purpose that explains it are mismatched or discrepant (e.g. one person justifies killing another for the purpose of getting the latter's gym shoes). With the step back, however, life is absurd because we lack a standard of evaluation in light of which we are nonarbitrarily able to justify taking seriously the purposes that we have in life. Thus, there is no nonarbitrary, final answer to questions about the seriousness with which we embrace the purposes that explain our pursuits in life. From Nagel's perspective, "[t]here does not appear to be any conceivable world (containing us) about which unsettlable doubts [concerning these purposes and the seriousness with which we take them] could not arise" (Nagel 2000, 181). And this is ultimately what makes life absurd. There is a noneliminable discrepancy between the need to have a final nonarbitrary answer (in the form of a standard of evaluation) to the regress of questions about the seriousness with which we approach our lives and the unavailability of such an answer. All of us are such that we will always take our purposes seriously without being able to provide a regress-stopping, rationally convincing answer for why we do so. This inability is, concludes Nagel, just part and parcel of the human predicament. And this would be the case in any world we might inhabit, even one in which all of our desires were fulfilled and purposes achieved. But this philosophical absurdity is not something that either calls for heroism in fighting or should produce despair. It is just part of the irony of being human that our lives are ultimately absurd or meaningless in the way described.

Perfect happiness

With the contributions of Taylor, Sartre, and Nagel as a backdrop, I develop in this section a position on the meaning of life that will make clear what I will assume is being asked when someone like my cousin queries "What is the meaning of life?" To develop this position, it is necessary first to clarify the concepts of an intrinsic and an instrumental good. "Good" (like "evil") is a value concept, and to say that something is intrinsically good is to say that it is good in value on its own or in itself, where "good on its own" and "good in itself" mean something like "it is good and its goodness is not explained by the goodness of anything else." Similarly, something is intrinsically evil if it is evil in value on its own or in itself and, therefore, its evilness is not explained by the evilness of anything else.

Corresponding to the concept of an intrinsic good (evil) is the idea of an instrumental good (evil). An instrumental good (evil) is one whose goodness (evilness) is explained by the goodness (evilness) of something else. In the case of an instrumental good, its goodness is ultimately explained either by the intrinsic good to which it gives rise or the intrinsic evil that it prevents, diminishes, or eliminates. An instrumental evil ultimately derives its evilness from either the intrinsic evil to which it gives rise or the intrinsic good that it prevents, diminishes, or eliminates. Given that something is good (evil), instrumental good (evil), and intrinsic good (evil) are logically related concepts in the sense that the concept of an intrinsic good (evil) is the logical opposite of an instrumental good (evil) (however, see the addendum at the end of this chapter). If something is good but not intrinsically good, then it is instrumentally good (and vice versa), and if something is evil but not intrinsically evil, then it is instrumentally evil (and vice versa). From here on, to avoid repetition and the constant use of parentheses, I will, for the most part, discuss intrinsic and instrumental value properties only in terms of goodness.

Given the concept of an intrinsic good, how is it related to the idea of an ultimate or final purpose, goal, or end? The relationship is fairly straightforward. An ultimate purpose or final goal for a person is an intrinsic good, and this entails that an individual pursues that purpose or goal for its own sake. Thus, if X is good and a purpose or goal that one is seeking, it can be asked whether one is pursuing X as a means to something else, Y, which is good. If one is, then one is thinking of X as an instrumental good and not as an intrinsic good. It is an instrumental good because it is sought as a means to Y. Of Y, it can now be asked whether it is sought as a means to something else, Z, which is good. If it is, then it too is an instrumental good. If Z is pursued for its own sake, and not as a means to anything else, then it is a final or ultimate goal and is an intrinsic good.

One other relationship involving intrinsic goodness needs clarification. This is the relationship between what is intrinsically good and desire. Many, if not most, people who have thought about the relationship between desire and what is of value have concluded that desire and goodness are conceptually linked in the sense that desire is ultimately and in principle directed at obtaining something that is intrinsically good (and in avoiding what is intrinsically evil). Stated slightly differently, if something is desired for its own sake, then it is intrinsically good. Given that this is the case and an instrumental good is a means to an intrinsic good, desire for an instrumental good is rooted in and intelligible in the light of a desire for the intrinsic good to which that instrumental good is a means.

With the idea of an intrinsic good and ultimate purpose in hand, we can revisit and assess Nagel's analysis of the meaning of life, which I summarized in the previous section. According to Nagel, each of us inevitably takes his or her life seriously insofar as we take seriously the purposes that justify our pursuits in life, and we inevitably step back and ask about these purposes "Am I justified in taking them seriously?" Nagel claims that what ultimately makes life absurd is the fact that this question has no satisfactory (nonarbitrary) answer because we lack a nonarbitrary standard of evaluation in light of which to formulate an answer. The only way to terminate the asking of the question is arbitrarily to draw a line and say "Thus far and no further." But contrary to what Nagel argues, if something is intrinsically good and, therefore, rightly pursued for its own sake, then it is reasonable to maintain that at some point the correct answer to Nagel's question must be as follows: "I am justified in taking this purpose in life seriously because the purpose that I am taking seriously concerns or is about what is intrinsically good. Taking this purpose that concerns what is intrinsically good seriously requires no further justification. Indeed, I would be unreasonable were I not to take this purpose seriously. Hence, in this case there is nothing in the least bit arbitrary about my taking what I do seriously, given the fact that what I take seriously concerns what is intrinsically good. Moreover, it is reasonable to believe that life is meaningful because of the attainment of an ultimate purpose that I take seriously."

Life is not, therefore, as Nagel argues, inescapably, ultimately absurd or meaningless. As another philosopher Paul Edwards states, "It makes sense for a person to ask about something 'Is it really worthwhile?' or 'Is it really worth the trouble?' if he does not regard it as intrinsically valuable.... It does not make sense [however] to ask such a question about something he regards as valuable in its own right [intrinsically good]" (Edwards 2000, 141). Perhaps Edwards' point concerning the senselessness of a question about troubling oneself with what is intrinsically good can be teased out in the following way. Nagel seems to believe that if one can step back and ask a question about taking something seriously, then the question is thereby appropriate or warranted. But why think this is the case? After all, one can ask "What is the color of the number three?", but asking the question does not make it appropriate. "How long have you been beating your wife?" is certainly a question, but thoroughly unwarranted when posed to a man who has never physically abused his spouse. It is sometimes asked about God's existence "Who created God?" However, if God is a necessary being (a being that cannot not exist and, therefore, never came into existence), then the question presupposes something about God (that God came into existence) that is not true. Similarly, "What is my justification for taking X seriously?" might or might not be a sensible question. It all depends on what is substituted for "X." If X is intrinsically good, then to ask what the justification is for taking it seriously is seriously misguided. When it comes to what is intrinsically good, no justification is needed for taking it seriously.

If the foregoing is a reasonable response to Nagel's analysis of the meaning of life, and I believe that it is, then it is only natural to ask what is intrinsically good. For the beginning of an answer to this question, I once again turn to Nagel:

> I think pleasure and pain are very important, and that they provide a clearer case for a certain kind of objective value than preferences and desires .... I shall defend the unsurprising claim

that sensory pleasure is good and pain bad, no matter whose they are…. Almost everyone takes the avoidance of his own pain and the promotion of his own pleasure as subjective reasons for action in a fairly simple way; they are not backed up by any further reasons. (Nagel 1986, 156)

It is not much of a stretch to understand Nagel as claiming that pleasure is intrinsically good and pain is intrinsically evil, and that given their status as such each of us seeks to promote his or her own experiences of pleasure for their own sake and to avoid experiences of pain for their own sake. This is fairly simple. What I believe is also fairly simple is the idea of an unending life (existence) that is filled with the best possible or optimal experiences of pleasure (assuming that there are such optimal experiences) and without any experiences of pain. Such a life is the happiest life possible. In other words, without much effort at all, a person uses the ideas of pleasure and pain to form the idea of his or her own optimal well-being, which is the idea of perfect or complete happiness, where this happiness extends indefinitely into the future and consists of nothing but experiences of pleasure. So, maximal well-being, which is perfect happiness, consists of nothing but conscious psychological states of a certain kind, namely, pleasures.

To bolster Nagel's implicit and my explicit claims about pleasure and happiness, I turn to two theists. First, consider some thoughts of Augustine about pleasure and happiness. In his *Confessions*, Book X.21, Augustine asks how it is that we come by our concept of happiness. He notes that even when he is sad he can recall pleasure, just as he can recall happiness when he is unhappy (Augustine 1961, 227; here I follow Gareth Matthews' (2005, 145) translation of the Latin word *gaudium* as "pleasure" and not "joy," because, as Matthews says, in this context "joy" sounds too pious and not robustly experiential). Moreover, Augustine says that everyone agrees on wanting to be happy in the same way that they would agree on wanting to experience pleasure. In fact, says Augustine, they call this pleasure "happiness." And although one person achieves pleasure from this and another obtains it from that, each aims to experience pleasure. Because everyone has experienced some pleasure, Augustine says their minds turn to pleasure whenever they hear of the state or life of "happiness" (Augustine 1961, 228).

The philosopher Terry Eagleton agrees with Augustine that happiness is usually associated with pleasure. About a woman who is determined to become an actress but is anxious, dispirited, and lives on a pittance, he says "[s]he is not what we would usually call happy. Her life is not pleasant or enjoyable" (Eagleton 2007, 81). But Eagleton believes this connection between happiness and pleasure is problematic because "pleasure is a passing sensation, while happiness at its best is an enduring condition of being. You can experience intense pleasure without being the least happy" (Eagleton 2007, 83). Surely, however, this alleged problem is not real. Assuming pleasures are passing, a happy life is one filled with such pleasures, and a perfectly happy life is one that never ends and is filled with nothing but such pleasures. If such a life were to last for a short period of time, then it would be a happy life while it lasted. Obviously, the longer it lasts, the better. Can one, as Eagleton says, experience intense pleasure and not be the least bit happy? Well, it all depends upon what else is going on in one's life. If in addition to the experience of intense pleasure one's life is filled with much pain, then one is surely not happy *overall*, though it is true to say that one is happy *with respect to* the intense pleasure.

The second theist whose thoughts about happiness and pleasure are worth considering is the Oxford/Cambridge medievalist C. S. Lewis. In a letter written to Canon Oliver Chase Quick, who had written to Lewis about his (Lewis') book *The Problem of Pain*, Lewis says "I think *all* pleasure simply good: what we call bad pleasures are pleasures produced by actions, or inactions, [which] break the moral law, and it is those actions or inactions [which] are bad, not the pleasures" (Lewis 2004, 462–3). Lewis is explicit about the intrinsic goodness of pleasure (and intrinsic evilness of pain) when he writes "I have no doubt at all that pleasure in itself is a good and pain in itself an evil" (Lewis 1967, 21). And Lewis' belief in the link between happiness and experiences of pleasure is evidenced by the following remark: "Huge pleasures ... sometimes (if we are careless) not even acknowledged or remembered, invade us from [real, lived life]. Hence the unreasonable happiness which sometimes surprises a man at those very hours which ought, according to all objective rules, to have been the most miserable" (Lewis 1986, 53). In the just-mentioned letter to Canon Quick, Lewis goes on to add that "I [would] say that every pleasure (even the lowest) is a likeness to, even, in its restricted mode, a foretaste of, the end for [which] we exist, the fruition [enjoyment] of God" (Lewis 2004, 463). In light of his belief that the enjoyment of God is the end for which we exist and that this end is perfect or complete happiness, Lewis says that "God not only understands but *shares* ... the desire for complete and ecstatic happiness. He made me for no other purpose than to enjoy it" (Lewis 2004, 123). According to Lewis, complete or ecstatic happiness is the life of the blessed and we must suppose "the life of the blessed to be an end in itself, indeed The End" (Lewis 1992, 92).

In light of the thoughts of Nagel, Augustine, and Lewis about pleasure and happiness, I will assume from this point on that happiness and the pleasures that compose it are intrinsically good. Given that this is the case and it is true that anyone who desires to be happy takes having a happy life seriously, Nagel's question "Am I justified in taking this purpose seriously?" receives an affirmative answer, because happiness is intrinsically good and desirable for its own sake. Anyone who did not take his or her own happiness seriously would require a justification for not doing so. Indeed, there is no better candidate for absurdity than a life wherein one does not take one's own happiness seriously.

Now, consider Taylor's treatment of the meaning of life. He suggests that a meaningful life is one in which one has a desire and is able to fulfill or satisfy it. A purpose, goal, or end is an object of a desire (that at which a desire is directed), and the achievement of that purpose makes for meaningfulness. What is the object of desire? If we take Taylor's discussion of Sisyphus literally, the object of desire is an action. In the case of Sisyphus, the action is that of rolling a stone. For human beings, the action might be working a job, raising a family, or a host of other actions. But is desire fundamentally directed at action? If pleasure is the ultimate object of desire, the answer is "No," and we get a different picture of meaningfulness than that which is suggested by Taylor. For example, Nagel says the following about physical pleasure: "Physical pleasure and pain do not usually depend on activities or desires which themselves raise questions of justification and value. They are just sensory experiences in relation to which we are fairly passive, but toward which we feel involuntary desire or aversion" (Nagel 1986, 156). In other words, physical pleasures (pleasures that have physical sources) are experiences with respect to which we are essentially patients and not agents. Stated slightly differently, experiences of pleasures are not actions that we perform. Nagel also says that physical pleasures do not usually depend on activities that themselves raise questions of justification and value. It is not clear to me what Nagel means by this statement. After all, if pleasure is intrinsically good, then any action that leads to it has instrumental value in the form of being instrumentally good. Similar points can be made for mental pleasures. If one derives experiences of pleasure from philosophizing, reading, solving mathematical puzzles, etc., then it is true to say that those experiences can be produced by and accompany actions that are instrumentally good in virtue of this productive relationship, even though the experiences themselves are passions and not actions. Moreover, because experiences of pleasure constitute happiness, if one is happy through performing actions, then actions produce happiness, even though happiness is itself not an action. Hence, if Sisyphus desired to roll rocks, he desired to do so because he received pleasure from doing so. Ultimately, Sisyphus' desire must have been directed at experiencing pleasure that is intrinsically good, and his goal of experiencing this pleasure was the purpose that justified his performing an action (rolling a stone) that produced that experience.

The philosopher Robert Nozick raises a well-known challenge to the view that a meaningful life essentially consists in experiences of pleasure (Nozick 1974, 42–5). He asks us to consider a hypothetical experience machine to which one can connect in order to have any experiences that one wants. By hypothesis, we can assume that the experiences one wants are nothing but experiences of pleasure. Moreover, all the time that one is connected to the machine, which we can suppose in the present context is forever, one will not have to do anything. One will never have to act. As a patient, one will simply be infused with experiences of pleasure. Nozick's question is this: would a reasonable person choose to connect to the machine? He believes that no reasonable person would connect to the machine, because a meaningful life is one in which an individual *does* certain things in order to *be* a certain kind of person.

Given my views of pleasure and happiness, it is incumbent upon me to explain why I believe a reasonable person would connect to the experience machine, were such an option available. But my explanation will have to wait until later chapters when I will have completed more of the philosophical groundwork that I will need to take up the matter in a more informed way. So, I issue a promissory note here that I will redeem later.

I now turn to Sartre, who believes that a meaningful life requires that the subject of that life be an artifact created by an artificer. Can Sartre's view contribute anything to the view of a meaningful life that I have developed so far? I believe that it can. For the sake of discussion, let us assume that I (and you) have been created by God (the artisan) for a purpose. What might that purpose be? Well, it is not too much of a stretch, if it is a stretch at all, to suppose that the purpose for which I am created is that I experience perfect happiness. After all, I desire that I be perfectly happy and I desire nothing else more deeply or fundamentally than this. As Augustine said, "For who wishes anything for any other reason than that he may become happy? ... It is the decided opinion of all who use their brains that all men desire to be happy" (Augustine 1993, IV. 23; X.1). Nothing could really be more obvious.

If a human being is an artifact that is created by God for the purpose that he or she experience perfect happiness, then it is plausible to say that an individual is perfected or made perfect by the experience of pleasure. But one must be careful here. What one must not think is that pleasures are good because it is human nature to want and experience them. As the philosopher Daniel Haybron writes:

> [I]t is not as if we *make* pleasure good in wanting it, as if pleasure were itself neither good nor bad—as if our preference for pleasure, rather than displeasure, were arbitrary. I do not mean arbitrary in the sense that there could be no explanation of any sort for it. The idea is rather that, if pleasure is not intrinsically good, then we ultimately have no more reason to like it [as an] experience ... than to dislike it. We could just as well have been constructed to want experiences of extreme nausea or depression rather than massages and happiness, and *there would be no non-instrumental reason for preferring the one constitution to the latter.* This is hard to believe. (Haybron 2008, 188)

In short, experiences of pleasure perfect an individual and God made us for the purpose that we exist forever and experience nothing but pleasure, because pleasure is intrinsically good. It is because experiences of pleasure are intrinsically good that we are better off or perfected by having them.

I close this section by making one final point. The claim that pleasure is intrinsically good is not the claim that pleasure is *morally* good. Rather, it is the claim that pleasure is good in a real but *nonmoral* ("non-moral" means "neither moral nor immoral" and not "immoral") way. "Good" is a value term and a genus that divides into two species of value, which are the "moral" and the "non-moral." Moreover, it is because pleasure is good in the nonmoral sense that we have moral good. Roughly speaking, moral good is a feature of *actions* that are performed either in order to produce experiences of pleasure or in order to eliminate or prevent experiences of pain (and moral evil is a feature of actions that are performed either in order to produce experiences of pain or in order to eliminate or prevent experiences of pleasure), whereas nonmoral good is, as I have already indicated, a feature of *experiences* with respect to which we are passive (it is a feature of *passions*). Given that pleasure is desired for its own sake, it follows that desire is ultimately directed at an intrinsic good that is nonmoral in nature. The distinction between moral and nonmoral good is important and I will refer to it again in future chapters.

A plausible understanding of "What is the meaning of life?"

In light of the discussion in the previous section, I believe it is plausible to understand the question "What is the meaning of life?" (which is question (1) at the outset of the second section of this chapter) as the question "What is the ultimate (final or all-encompassing) purpose for which I exist?" Moreover, after examining the views of Taylor, Sartre, and Nagel, I believe that the fairly simple and direct answer to this question is that I exist for the ultimate purpose (from here on, I will feel free to include or leave out the word "ultimate" from "ultimate purpose") that I experience the intrinsic goodness of perfect happiness, where this experience satisfies my deepest desire and constitutes my well-being. In what immediately follows, I briefly explain how this answer draws upon and relates to the thoughts of these three philosophers about the meaning of life.

First, consider Taylor's contribution. As he suggests, meaningfulness involves a desire, the object of that desire (which is a goal or purpose), and the satisfaction of that desire (which is the achievement of the goal). With these ideas in hand, we can say with respect to one's life as a whole (which is the subject of the question "Why do I exist?") that one has the desire for perfect happiness and the satisfaction of that desire makes for an ultimately meaningful life. The failure to achieve that satisfaction (e.g. because of the failure to forever eliminate experiences of pain) entails that one's life is ultimately not fully meaningful and to some degree or other (e.g. depending on the amount and intensity of the ineliminable experiences of pain) meaningless or absurd. From here on, I will refer to this absurdity as simply "ultimate absurdity."

The experience of perfect happiness is the purpose for which each of us exists. The problem, however, is that perfect happiness is not to be had in this life. Where does this leave us? Lewis writes, "If I find in myself a desire which no experience in this world can satisfy, the most probable explanation is that I was made for another world. If none of my earthly pleasures satisfy it, that does not prove that the universe is a fraud" (Lewis 2001a, 136–7). True enough. But were we never able to satisfy this desire, then the universe would ultimately be a fraud (absurd). The following comment by Jeffrey Gordon sums up our situation perfectly: "[W]e have in addition to our worldly aspirations, aspirations of a transcendental order, and if the world is simply dumb to such needs, our condition is surely ludicrous. An earnest seeker flitting in a void, our condition would comprise the Absurd" (Gordon 1984, 27).

Second, there is Nagel's concern about taking our purposes seriously. Given that perfect happiness is intrinsically good, it is perfectly reasonable for one to take the purpose of experiencing one's own perfect happiness seriously. Thus, Nagel's claim that life is ultimately absurd because no nonarbitrary answer can be given to the question "But why should I take this purpose in life seriously?" is mistaken.

And, finally, we have Sartre's thought about artificers and artifacts. In terms of perfect happiness, it is perfectly reasonable for one to hold that the purpose for which one is created by God is that one experience perfect happiness. The desire for this happiness illuminates the purpose for which one is made by one's artificer.

The French philosopher Albert Camus is famous for claiming that "there is but one truly serious philosophical problem, and that is suicide" (Camus 2000, 94). Why does Camus say this? Though his argument for this claim is at times difficult to follow, the gist of it seems to be that each of us longs for clarity in the form of understanding why it is that he or she exists. In other words, the question of suicide arises because we desire to understand the world and our place in it, but the world does not cooperate insofar as it fails to provide us with an answer that satisfies this desire. "People despair of true knowledge," writes Camus (Camus 2000, 98), and they turn to religion in light of this despair (they make a leap of faith) with the hope that all will be well in the end, even though the understanding that they crave is not forthcoming in this life.

From what I have argued so far in this chapter, if life is ultimately absurd, it is not for the reason that Camus gives. If I am right, we do not lack the understanding that Camus insists we lack. The world has not failed to inform us about the purpose of our existence. Rather, the purpose is obvious and well understood: each of us exists for the purpose of being perfectly happy. My view of life's meaning locates the potential for ultimate absurdity in the existence of that purpose and the failure to have it accomplished. The threat of ultimate absurdity does not arise with a desire for a knowledge that we might not be able to have but with a desire for perfect happiness that we might not be able to satisfy.

A plausible understanding of "What makes life meaningful?"

"What makes life meaningful?" is question (2) at the outset of the second section of this chapter. At that time, I suggested that a plausible reading of question (2) is "What makes life worth living?" In light of the earlier discussion of the concept of intrinsic goodness, it seems eminently reasonable to hold that what makes life worth living is the experience of what is intrinsically good, and that a life that is most worth living is one in which one's experience of this good is maximal in nature. I have argued that the maximal experience of this good is perfect happiness. So, the most plausible answer to the question "What makes life worth living?" is the simple answer "Happiness," and the answer to "What ultimately makes life worth living?" is "Perfect happiness, where perfect happiness, as that which consists of nothing but experiences of pleasure and constitutes one's well-being, is the purpose for which one is created by God."

Euthyphro's objection

Pleasure is intrinsically good and so is the perfect happiness that is composed of nothing but experiences of pleasure. In his justly famous dialogue *Euthyphro*, Plato (through the mouth of Socrates) asks the following question: "Is the pious loved by the gods because it is pious, or is it pious because it is loved?" (Plato 1998a, 52) Because I am presently concerned with pleasure and happiness, and not piety, I will rephrase Socrates' question as follows: "Is pleasure loved by the gods because it is good, or is it good because it is loved?" If pleasure is intrinsically good, the correct answer to this question is that pleasure is loved by the gods because it is intrinsically good. Now, consider one more rephrasing of Socrates' question: "Is pleasure declared by the gods to be good because it is good, or is it good because they declare it to be so?" Given the meaning of "intrinsic good," pleasure is not good because it is declared so by the gods. Were that the case, then pleasure would be good in virtue of its relationship to something else, which contradicts the concept of what it is for something to be intrinsically good.

Because the goodness of pleasure is intrinsic in nature, pleasure's goodness is not explained by what anyone, divine or human, says. Thus, if God says that pleasure is good, this is because it is intrinsically good and He knows it to be so. Some theists will contest this position about pleasure's goodness, because in their view it undermines God's omnipotence or all-powerfulness. According to them, if God were to say that pleasure is intrinsically evil and pain is intrinsically good, then that would be the case. Hence, it is just wrong to say that pleasure is intrinsically good.

For a rebuttal, I turn to C. S. Lewis who, as I have already pointed out, believed that pleasure is intrinsically good. Lewis writes that "[God's] omnipotence means power to do all that is intrinsically possible, not to do the intrinsically impossible" (Lewis 1962, 28). Because pleasure is intrinsically good, it is impossible that it ever be in and of itself either not good or evil. To claim that pleasure might be either intrinsically not good or evil is nonsense. As Lewis says, "[M]eaningless combinations of words do not suddenly acquire meaning simply because we prefix to them the two other words 'God can,'" and "nonsense remains nonsense even when we talk it about God" (Lewis 1962, 28). If this were not the case, then God could both make Himself exist and not exist at the same time, or make Himself simultaneously perfectly morally good and perfectly morally evil. At this point, we have reached and crossed over the border into the land of logical absurdity.

A plausible understanding of "Is life meaningful?"

Question (3), which I introduced at the outset of the second section of this chapter, is "Is life meaningful?" There, I stated that a plausible understanding of the question is "Does life make any sense in terms of things fitting together in an intelligible way?" Given the discussion up to this point in the chapter, the "things" that need to fit together in an intelligible way include, first and foremost, the desire for perfect happiness and the fulfillment of it by experiences of pleasure that are intrinsically good. Other "things" that need to fit together in an intelligible way with the fulfillment of this desire include moral actions (e.g. should one have experiences of pleasure, regardless of how one chooses to act, whether morally or immorally?). How and whether experiences of pleasure and moral actions can be fit together intelligibly is something that will require much discussion at various points in subsequent chapters (e.g. Chapters 2 and 5). If they ultimately cannot be fit together in an intelligible way, then life will end up being ultimately and deeply absurd.

C. S. Lewis begins his book *The Problem of Pain* with the following autobiographical remarks about why he believed that God did not exist:

> Not many years ago when I was an atheist, if anyone asked me, "Why do you not believe in God?" my reply would have run something like this: "Look at the universe we live in. By far the greatest part of it consists of empty space, completely dark and unimaginably cold. The bodies which move in this space are so few and so small in comparison with the space itself that even if

every one of them were known to be crowded as full as it could
hold with perfectly happy creatures, it would still be difficult to
believe that life and happiness were more than a by-product to
the power that made the universe. As it is, however, the scientists
think it likely that very few of the suns of space—perhaps none
of them except our own—have any planets; and in our own
system it is improbable that any planet except the Earth sustains
life. And Earth herself existed without life for millions of years
and may exist for millions more when life has left her." (Lewis
1962, 13)

As an atheist, Lewis seems to have believed that God does not
exist because life is absurd, and life is absurd because of a disparity
between the spatial and temporal properties exhibited by us and
those exhibited by the universe. Because space is for the most part
an empty, dark, and cold backdrop to our lives, our lives must
ultimately also be largely empty, dark, and cold (any happiness
they contain being no more than an accident). And because the
duration of our lives is ever so brief in comparison with that of the
earth and the universe, our lives must be ultimately insignificant.
Echoing Lewis, Nagel points out that many seek to convince us
that life is ultimately absurd by noting that "we are tiny specks in
the infinite vastness of the universe; our lives are mere instants even
on a geological time scale, let alone a cosmic one" (Nagel 2000,
177). Nagel goes on to insist that these points about space and time
cannot be the explanation for why life is ultimately absurd, if it is
so. At best, they can be used to convey the reality of an ultimate
absurdity whose roots lie elsewhere. After all, adds Nagel, "if our
lives are absurd given our present size, why would they be any less
absurd if we filled the universe (either because we were larger or
because the universe was smaller)?" (Nagel 2000, 177). And if we
lived forever, wouldn't it merely follow that a life that is absurd for
70 or 80 years is also absurd for an eternity?

Lewis' remarks that I quoted above are autobiographical in
nature and were written when he was a Christian reflecting back
on his earlier life as an atheist. Like Nagel, he too came to believe
that considerations of space in and of themselves explain nothing
about the ultimate absurdity of life or the lack thereof. According
to Lewis, this is because matters of size have nothing to do with
matters of value. Thus, there is

no reason why the minute earth and the yet smaller human creatures upon it should not be the most important things in a universe that contains the spiral nebulae.... If size and value had any real connexion, small differences in size would accompany small differences in value as surely as large differences in size accompany large differences in value. But no sane man could suppose that this is so. I don't think the taller man *slightly* more valuable than the shorter one. I don't allow a slight superiority to trees over men, and then neglect it because it is too small to bother about. I perceive, as long as I am dealing with the small differences of size, that they have no connexion with value whatsoever. I therefore conclude that the importance attached to the great differences of size is an affair, not of reason but of emotion .... (Lewis 1970, 40–1)

Lewis came to see that issues about the meaningfulness or absurdity of life in the sense expressed by the question "Is life meaningful?" are fundamentally issues about value, not matters of space and time *per se*. If I am right in what I have written so far and will elaborate upon in subsequent chapters, these issues of value will fundamentally concern the matter of perfect happiness. But given the centrality of the concept of perfect happiness, considerations of time at least do not end up being completely irrelevant to avoiding a deeply absurd life. For example, given that the purpose of life is that one experience the intrinsic goodness of perfect happiness and there cannot be any reason why one would wish for that experience to cease once it had commenced (I will have more to say about this issue in Chapter 2), one must conclude that if perfect happiness is experienced in time, then it must be a state of existence without end.

This world, the afterlife, and the soul

Earlier, I explained how desire is ultimately directed at what is intrinsically good. Given that what is good for an individual is his or her own experience of the intrinsic goodness of perfect happiness, it is the case that a person's desire is ultimately aimed at his or her own perfect happiness. I regard this point as fairly obvious. Just as obvious, it seems to me, is a fact I briefly noted earlier, which is that

perfect happiness is not to be found in this life. Once again, I turn
to Augustine for support:

> As for those who have supposed that the sovereign good ... [is]
> to be found in this life, and have placed it either in the soul or the
> body, or in both, or, to speak more explicitly, either in pleasure or
> in virtue, or in both; in repose or in virtue, or in both; in pleasure
> and repose, or in virtue, or in all combined; in the primary objects
> of nature, or in virtue, or in both—all these have, with a marvelous
> shallowness, sought to find their blessedness in this life and in
> themselves. Contempt has been poured upon such ideas ....
> For what flood of eloquence can suffice to detail the miseries
> of this life? ... For when, where, how, in this life can these
> primary objects of nature be possessed so that they may not be
> assailed by unforeseen accident? Is the body of the wise man
> exempt from any pain which may dispel pleasure, from any
> disquietude which may banish repose? The amputation or decay
> of the members of the body puts an end to its integrity, deformity
> blights its beauty, weakness its health, lassitude its vigour,
> sleepiness or sluggishness its activity—and which of these is it
> that may not assail the flesh of the wise man? Comely and fitting
> attitudes and movements of the body are numbered among the
> prime natural blessings; but what if some sickness makes the
> members tremble? What if a man suffers from curvature of
> the spine to such an extent that his hands reach the ground, and
> he goes upon all-fours like a quadruped? Does not this destroy
> all beauty and grace in the body, whether at rest or in motion?
> What shall I say of the fundamental blessings of the soul, sense
> and intellect, of which the one is given for the perception, and the
> other for the comprehension of truth? But what kind of sense is
> it that remains when a man becomes deaf and blind? Where are
> reason and intellect when disease makes a man delirious? We can
> scarcely, or not at all, refrain from tears, when we think of or see
> the actions and words of such frantic persons, and consider how
> different from and even opposed to their own sober judgment
> and ordinary conduct their present demeanour is. (Augustine
> 1993, XIX.4)

In short, if perfect happiness is to be realized and the desire for it
satisfied, there must be another life where this is possible. Moreover,

the possibility of experiencing perfect happiness in another life presupposes that one is able to survive death. It has been the view of most people that a necessary condition for the survival of death is that one be or have a soul that is separate from its physical body and capable of surviving the demise of the latter.

It is not surprising that those who scoff at the idea that God exists and created us for a purpose like that of being perfectly happy also deride the idea of the afterlife. For example, Baggini writes that "[b]elief in life after death can only be based on faith, since the evidence and good reasons required for a rational argument that it exists are lacking. The only evidence we have for life after death is the testimony of those who claim to have seen or communicated with the dead" (Baggini 2004, 51). He adds that "[w]e are tied to our bodies much too intimately for it to be plausible that we are essentially immaterial souls temporarily inhabiting them. This is most evident when one considers the necessary link between thought and brain activity" (Baggini 2004, 52). Baggini believes that we are so closely tied to our bodies that we do not have freedom of the will in the sense that we are able to and actually do make causally undetermined choices. As he sees things, all of our actions are determined:

But the problem is that we seem to live in a universe where every physical event has a physical cause. Furthermore, there is what is known as the "causal closure of the physical domain", meaning everything within the physical world is caused by physical events and nothing else.... Put these facts together and a surprising conclusion follows: all our actions must be caused entirely by events in the physical world. And because physical causation is deterministic—which means that causes necessitate their effects in some way—that leaves no room for free will. (Baggini 2004, 118–19)

I will spend a good bit of time in Chapter 4 stating and examining an argument that is supposed to convince us of what Baggini calls "the causal closure of the physical domain." Not surprisingly, I will conclude that the argument fails and that there is room for freedom of the will in the sense that we are agents who make undetermined choices that causally produce events in the physical world for which there are no determining physical causes. However, because one can only do so much in a book like this, I do not have the space to argue explicitly against the position that we are merely material beings and for the view that we are or have souls (the soul exists), which from early childhood on is the natural way of looking at the world (Bloom 2004). For now, it will suffice to point out that if we have indeterministic freedom of the will, then there is not, contrary to what Baggini says, a necessary link between all thought and brain activity, where what happens in the brain determines what happens to our thought. On those occasions when we make causally undetermined choices, what happens in the brain is determined by how we choose. And if this is the case when we choose, then we have some evidence for the independence of our mental life from our bodily life.

I have argued elsewhere (Goetz 2005, 2011a, 2011b; see also Taliaferro 1994) that there is nothing incoherent or decisively problematic with the idea that the soul exists. Indeed, many who deny the existence of the soul concede that from the first-person, introspective point of view, which is the view from which it seems that we have indeterministic freedom of the will and that perfect happiness is the purpose of life, we are not aware of ourselves having any substantial parts (see Nagel 1986; McGinn 1991). That is, we do not seem to ourselves to be complex beings or entities that have parts. What I mean by this is the following: When we consider macro entities, such as tables, chairs, and our own bodies, and micro entities, such as cells and molecules, we realize that all of them are divisible into two or more parts. Even if, by hypothesis, we lacked the ability to divide one or more of these entities into parts, with the requisite instruments or tools this division would be possible. When we consider ourselves, however, we are not aware of ourselves being entities of a kind that are divisible into substantive parts.

As I say, many who deny the existence of the soul are willing to concede that we are not aware of ourselves having any substantial parts. However, for many who believe in the soul's existence, there is a stronger point to be made, which is that we are aware of ourselves lacking any substantial parts. According to these believers in the soul, while each of us is aware of himself or herself having multiple psychological capacities, these capacities are not and do not presuppose the existence of substantive parts that, when joined together, make up our selves. The philosopher René Descartes expresses this point as follows:

[I]n the first place ... there is a great difference between mind and body, inasmuch as body is by nature always divisible, and the mind is entirely indivisible. For, as a matter of fact, when I consider the mind, that is to say, myself inasmuch as I am only a thinking thing, I cannot distinguish in myself any parts, but apprehend myself to be clearly one and entire; and although the whole mind seems to be united to the whole body, yet if a foot, or an arm, or some other part, is separated from my body, I am aware that nothing has been taken away from my mind. And the faculties of willing, feeling, conceiving, etc. cannot be properly speaking said to be its parts, for it is one and the same mind which employs itself in willing and in feeling and understanding. (Descartes 1967, I: 196)

In opposition to both the weaker and stronger claims about what is revealed concerning the self from the first-person point of view, some have sought to argue that self-awareness reveals a self with parts. For example, David Armstrong (Armstrong 1999, 23) uses some thoughts of Plato in an effort to support the view that the self does have parts. He points out that Plato argues in his *Republic* for the existence of parts of the soul from the fact that we are the subjects of and can consider acting for the purpose of fulfilling either one, but not both, of two competing desires: "But, I [Socrates] said, I once heard a story which I believe, that Leontius the son of Aglaion, on his way up from the Piraeus under the outer side of the northern wall, becoming aware of dead bodies that lay at the place of public execution at the same time felt a desire to see them and a repugnance and aversion...." (Plato 1961, *Republic* 439E).

Contrary to what Armstrong (and, perhaps, Plato) would have us believe, if these desires are parts of the self, then they are not substantive parts in the sense that they are substantial entities in their own right whose loss would entail a corresponding substantial diminishment in the size of the self. To see that this is the case, suppose that Socrates loses one or both of the desires to see the dead bodies and not to see them (the loss of a desire is not an uncommon experience that each of us has). Does Socrates experience a substantial loss of himself? Not in the least. *All* of him would remain after the loss of either or both of the desires. Socrates would have changed, but not in the sense that there would be less of him in a substantive sense because of a loss of parts. He will survive this kind of psychological change in his entirety. Therefore, we will need an argument other than the one brought forth by Armstrong from Plato to support the idea that the self has substantive parts.

As I have already indicated, there is no space in this book to present a rigorous defense of the existence of the soul. For now, it will suffice to say that Baggini is simply mistaken when he says that "the only evidence we have for life after death is the testimony of those who claim to have seen or communicated with the dead" (Baggini 2004, 51). Before we ever consider such testimony, we have the evidence provided by our own first-person introspective awareness that we are not identical with or completely determined by our physical bodies, which at least raises for consideration the idea that we might survive death.

From here on, then, I will simply assume in what follows that there are no good reasons for rejecting the idea that the soul exists. I stress that no particular argument that I make in the following chapters hinges on my demonstrating the existence of the soul. All of these arguments will simply presuppose that if life is to be meaningful in the sense that I have explained in this chapter, then there must be an afterlife the entrance into which requires the existence of the soul. Should there either not be an afterlife or the soul not exist, life would ultimately be meaningless.

Conclusion

There are, of course, a veritable host of objections to my proposed understanding of the meaning of life. The rest of this book is in a way a prolonged answer to these objections. By means of considering and answering these criticisms, I hope to refine and clarify the view that I have elaborated in this chapter. Therefore, without further delay, I turn to the task of setting forth and answering the objections that might be raised against my understanding of the meaning of life.

Addendum

In light of the distinction I made in the section "Perfect Happiness" between an intrinsic and an instrumental good (evil), the following question naturally arises: If something that is good and has its goodness in itself is an intrinsic good, then why isn't something, whose goodness is explained by the goodness of something else, an extrinsic good, and not an instrumental one? In other words, doesn't "extrinsic" mean "not intrinsic," and isn't "extrinsic" the logical opposite of "intrinsic" such that "not intrinsically good" means "extrinsically good"?

Strictly speaking, "extrinsic" is the term that is the logical opposite of "intrinsic," and perhaps an instrumental good is only one kind of extrinsic good. In the minds of some, another kind of extrinsic good is one whose goodness depends on its relationship to the goodness of that which produces it, as opposed to having its goodness explained by the goodness of that which it produces. For example, quite often theists assert that our world is good because God, who is good, caused it to exist (God created it; I will address the matter of God's goodness in Chapter 3.) Nevertheless, when most people think of an extrinsic good, they typically think of what is instrumental in nature. Thus, the philosopher Richard Kraut uses "noninstrumentally good" in place of "intrinsically good" because "[i]t is not clear what the contrast between intrinsic goodness and extrinsic goodness amounts to when 'intrinsic' is not used … interchangeably with 'noninstrumental'" (Kraut 2007, 6, footnote 6). Given my aims in this book, I will simply stipulate that "extrinsic good" means "instrumental good," while all the time recognizing that, strictly speaking, the terms are not synonymous.

2

Perfect happiness and its atheistic critics

Perfect happiness is not the meaning of life

I claimed in Chapter 1 that the experience of perfect happiness, which is the uninterrupted and unending experience of nothing but pleasure, is the meaning of life. Not surprisingly, various philosophers have questioned and challenged the truth of this claim. In this chapter, I consider an assortment of objections to this view that, on the face of it, seems so plausible.

The most straightforward objection is simply the denial of it: perfect happiness is not the meaning of life. The philosopher Owen Flanagan puts forth this objection:

Some philosophers distinguish between things that have some property—for example, value—intrinsically and things that have the property derivatively. Money is worthless until we make it worth something. Happiness is said to have worth in and of itself. Suppose this is true. Would it follow that a life with many happy times in it was worth living? Not necessarily. Properties of parts do not confer the property on the whole. My parts are small, I am large. Happy times, even many of them, might not constitute

> a worthwhile life. But I am skeptical in any case that a life's meaning could be intrinsic—could come from just being alive or from something that has value, no matter what. Life's meaning must derive from things other than just being alive. Happiness is probably one of the things that confers worth, but it is not enough. After all, one might perversely find happiness in evil things. Perhaps happiness is not necessary even. One might live a life largely devoid of happiness but still live a good and worthwhile life—even as seen from the subjective point of view. (Flanagan 2000, 199)

Flanagan is right: life's meaning must come from something other than simply being alive. While being alive is a necessary condition of life's having meaning, it is not sufficient. On the view I am defending, this something other is perfect happiness, where perfect happiness is intrinsically good. Flanagan recognizes that people like me claim that happiness has intrinsic value, namely, the value of being intrinsically good. If we think of a life as something that can have many happy times and, thereby, many instances of intrinsic value, Flanagan asserts that a life of nothing but happy times, what I have called perfect happiness, might not, contrary to what I have claimed, be intrinsically good. According to Flanagan, this is because a property (intrinsic goodness) of each of the parts (happy times) is not conferred on the whole that is made up of nothing but those parts. His example of a case is his physical body, where the whole does not possess a property shared by each of its parts. Each of the parts is small but the body of which they are parts is big. And Flanagan is surely correct about this. However, I am not presupposing or asserting the truth of the principle that always and everywhere a property of each of the parts of a whole is also a property of the whole. What does seem plausible is the claim that, while *in certain instances* a property of each of the parts is not also a property of the whole, in other instances it is. Whether or not a property of each part is a property of the whole depends upon the property in question. For example, consider a crosswalk made up of nothing but red bricks. Each of the bricks is red. Is it reasonable to conclude that the crosswalk as a whole is red? Yes. Similarly, it seems eminently reasonable to conclude that a life that is made up of nothing but instances of happiness that are intrinsically good is, as a whole, a life of perfect happiness that is both intrinsically good and, therefore, good for its subject.

What, then, is one to say about Flanagan's claim that a life largely devoid of happiness could still be a good and worthwhile life? Understood in one way, Flanagan's claim seems eminently reasonable. Understood in another way, it seems obviously false. What is the eminently reasonable understanding? Well, it could be that someone like Mother Teresa's life was good and worthwhile in the sense that her work brought bodily and spiritual good to others. In the terms defined in Chapter 1, Mother Teresa's life was instrumentally good and worthwhile *for others*. But was it good and worthwhile *for her* (what Flanagan calls the "subjective point of view")? This is a different matter. From what we now know, the answer would appear to be that it was not (and if it was not, this illustrates the way in which Flanagan's claim seems obviously false). Mother Teresa describes, in her private correspondence, how she lived for decades with darkness and pain in her soul and repeatedly pleaded with God to bring light (happiness) into that darkness:

> Your Grace, ... please pray specially for me that I may not spoil His work and that our Lord may show Himself—for there is such terrible darkness within me, as if everything was [sic] dead. It has been like this more or less from the time I started "the work." ... Pray for me—for within me everything is icy cold.—It is only that blind faith that carries me through for in reality to me all is darkness. As long as Our Lord has all the pleasure—I really do not count.... I understand a little the tortures of hell—without God. I have no words to express what I want to say, and yet ... knowingly and willingly I offered ... to pass even eternity in this terrible suffering, if this would give Him now a little more pleasure .... (Mother Teresa 2007, 149, 163, 172)

Beyond trying to understand what Mother Teresa went through, which was obviously not good for her, what is interesting for present purposes is that she was willing to endure years of darkness and, if we take her at her word, eternity, if it would give Jesus *pleasure*. It seems fair to infer that, in her mind, the experience of pleasure by her Lord would justify her plight. However, at no point did she seek for its own sake the darkness that at times almost overwhelmed her. As the editor of her writings, Brian

Kolodiejchuk, rightly points out, "Mother Teresa did not enjoy suffering for the sake of suffering" (Mother Teresa 2007, 175). No one could do that because pain is intrinsically evil and, therefore, we all avoid it for its own sake. But while pain is intrinsically evil and never sought for its own sake, it can, as Mother Teresa understood, be instrumentally good if it leads to the experience of pleasure, whether one's own or that of someone else. For herself, then, Mother Teresa's life was much less than fully meaningful. Only her own experience of pleasure could have rectified her situation. In order for her life to end up ultimately meaningful, she will have to experience in the afterlife the perfect happiness for which she longed but never had in this life.

Finally, Flanagan makes the important point that one might perversely find happiness in evil things. Presumably, what he has in mind here is that some people obtain happiness through perversely wicked actions. And surely this is the case. However, as C. S. Lewis pointed out in his statement about pleasures that I quoted in Chapter 1, bad pleasures are simply pleasures that are produced by bad actions. It is the actions that are bad, not the pleasures. So the happiness that is made up of pleasures that are derived from bad actions is good, even though its sources are bad.

There is a further issue, which is raised by Flanagan's statement about people obtaining happiness through perversely wicked actions, to which I will devote a good deal of attention later in this chapter and again in Chapter 5. This is the issue of justice and the idea that it is intrinsically bad or evil that someone might obtain a great good like happiness through perverse means, when it is the morally good person who deserves happiness. If the unjust individual ends up perfectly happy or much happier than or equally as happy as the just individual, then life seems deeply absurd in the sense discussed in Chapter 1 that things ultimately fail to fit together in an intelligible way. Stated slightly differently, if everyone ultimately ends up in the same condition (vz. dead) regardless of how they live their lives, then being moral does not necessarily lead to better well-being and indeed might undermine it. As a result, the question "Why should I be moral?" needs to be addressed.

An objection as equally straightforward as Flanagan's to the view that life's purpose is perfect happiness is presented by Daniel Haybron. He insists that not all pleasures contribute to happiness (not all pleasures are "happiness-making"), but on a view like mine

> all sorts of shallow, fleeting pleasures are made to count toward happiness. Yet such pleasures intuitively play no constitutive role in determining how happy a person is. One's enjoyment of eating crackers, hearing a good song, sexual intercourse, scratching an itch, solving a puzzle, playing football, and so forth need not have the slightest impact on one's level of happiness (though, of course, they may). I enjoy, get pleasure from, a cheeseburger, yet I am patently not happier *thereby*. Conversely for superficial pleasures. The problem does not concern the intensity of such pleasures: an orgasm may well be intensely pleasurable, yet still fail to *move* one, to make one any happier (consider anonymous or solitary sex). Might the brief duration of the event be misleading our intuitions here? Not likely: it is not just that any particular superficial pleasure seems irrelevant. Even the whole pattern of such pleasures over time appears to be. To be sure, we would expect someone who underwent an unrelenting succession of minor irritations not to be very happy at *the end of it all*. But this does not show the irritations themselves to be constitutive of one's (un)happiness; it reflects rather our expectation that these experiences will impact some deeper aspect of one's psychology, such as one's mood. Intuitively, the trouble seems to be that such pleasures don't reach "deeply" enough, so to speak. They just don't *get* to us; they flit through consciousness and that's the end of it. (Haybron 2008, 63)

Haybron's criticism is straightforward and the correct response to it is equally straightforward: at the time they occur, experiences of pleasure from eating a cheeseburger and a sexual orgasm do make one happier, even if ever so slightly, than one would be without them, provided that one would otherwise not have had equally or more pleasant experiences. Haybron believes that the view behind this response just cannot be right because the stated pleasures do not go deep enough; they do not impact deeper aspects of one's psychology, such as one's mood. But why should one be concerned about one's moods, if it is not for the reason that they impact one's experiences of pleasure (and pain)? As Haybron states elsewhere, "an individual who is in a depressed mood will likely find little pleasure in what happens, will tend to look on the dark side of things, and may more likely be saddened by negative events (Haybron 2008, 67). We care about deep aspects of our psychological being like moods only to the extent that they affect what is on the surface, and given a surface of nothing but pleasure, the absence of moods would not be the least bit disconcerting. Perhaps a life of nothing but pleasure must include a mood of optimism about the future, provided one believes that this quality of life will continue indefinitely into the future. But ultimately one will be concerned about such optimism only if it is a source of pleasure.

Paul Thagard is another philosopher who denies that happiness, and by implication perfect happiness, is the meaning of life (Thagard 2010). According to Thagard, what people aim at are goals and it is the aiming at and at least partial accomplishment of goals that provides meaning (Thagard 2010, 146, 165–6). Individuals are happy when they accomplish their goals, but happiness is no more than a product or result of goal satisfaction. It is not by itself a goal (Thagard 2010, 146).

In support of his claim that happiness is not by itself a goal, Thagard says that "[i]t is unclear how people could actually set themselves a reasonably achievable goal of being happy.... The only way you can set out to make yourself happy is to adopt goals whose satisfaction could then make you happy" (Thagard 2010, 146). "Of course," says Thagard, "someone could argue that goals ... are important only to the extent that their satisfaction makes you happy" (Thagard 2010, 146), with the implication being that happiness is by itself the ultimate goal. Of course, that seems to be the obvious response. However, Thagard appears to believe that because "happiness is an effect of satisfaction in other domains" (Thagard 2010, 147), it cannot by itself be the ultimate goal at which the satisfactions of subsidiary goals are aimed.

But why should the fact that happiness is an effect entail that it cannot be a goal? As I pointed out in Chapter 1, the experience of pleasure that constitutes happiness is not an action that we perform but a passion that we undergo. Therefore, there is nothing incoherent in the idea that happiness, which is not an action, is the ultimate goal at which the achievement of subsidiary goals by means of actions is aimed.

Perhaps, however, Thagard believes that the problem with happiness being the ultimate goal of our actions is of a different nature. As I quoted earlier, Thagard states that it is not clear how people could actually set for themselves a reasonably achievable goal of being happy. He goes on to quote Nathaniel Hawthorne's pithy quip that "Happiness is as a butterfly which, when pursued, is always beyond our grasp, but which if you will sit down quietly, may alight upon you" (Thagard 2010, 146). Two points in response are appropriate here.

First, Hawthorne's words confirm my point that happiness is an experience with respect to which we are essentially passive. Second, Thagard is rightly concerned that if happiness is a goal that is not achievable, then something is seriously amiss. Absurdity of a deep kind is present. His response to this problem is to deny that happiness is a goal. A different approach is to acknowledge what is obvious, which is that happiness is a goal (indeed perfect happiness is the ultimate goal), and to argue as I do in this book that it is reasonable to hold that it is achievable.

There are other reasons than those mentioned by Flanagan and Thagard for claiming that perfect happiness is not the meaning of life. For example, one might believe that perfect happiness is not life's meaning because the idea of perfect happiness is conceptually incoherent. This is the position of the philosopher Bernard Williams in his essay "The Makropulos Case: Reflections on the Tedium of Immortality" (Williams 1973). In summarizing and discussing Williams' essay, I draw heavily from John Martin Fischer's paper "Why Immortality Is Not So Bad" (Fischer 1994).

Williams sets forth two necessary conditions of immortality and its desirability: (1) that the future person must be the same as (numerically identical with) the individual concerned and (2) that the future life of that individual must be attractive to him in the sense that his future goals, projects, values, and interests must be suitably related to his present goals, projects, values, and interests. If they are not suitably related, then there is a risk that the individual will now find it difficult to regard those future goals, projects, values, and interests as sufficiently interesting to support a present desire that he have them as his own in the future.

Given that I am assuming (see the end of Chapter 1) that souls exist and are capable of surviving from this life into the next, condition (1) is fulfilled. What about condition (2)? Can it be fulfilled? Williams thinks not. With regard to condition (2), Williams poses a dilemma: Either an individual's fundamental desires, interests, purposes, and projects (his character) remain the same over time, or they do not. If they do remain the same, then, given that their number is finite, they will eventually be satisfied or fulfilled and boredom will ensue. If they do not remain the same (they change too much), then the individual's future desires, interests, purposes, and projects will not be similar enough to his present desires, interests, purposes, and projects to make him now desire to survive to be the subject of what is so different. The person will simply prefer to go out of existence.

What about the first alternative? As Fischer points out, there is a distinction between self-exhausting and repeatable pleasures. A self-exhausting pleasure is one that is associated with an activity the performance of which terminates any further need to do it again. An example Fischer provides is of an activity that you desire to do just once to prove to yourself that you can do it:

> Imagine ... that you are somewhat afraid of heights, and you have been working hard to overcome this phobia. You form the goal of climbing Mt Whitney just to show yourself that you have overcome the fear—just to show yourself that you can control your life and overcome obstacles. Upon climbing the mountain, you may in fact be very pleased and proud. Indeed, you may be deeply satisfied. But also you may have absolutely no desire to climb Mt Whitney (or any other mountain) again. You have accomplished your goal, but there is no impetus toward repeating the relevant activity or the pleasure that issues from it. (Fischer 1994, 262–3)

But as Fischer also notes, there is another kind of pleasure. There is repeatable pleasure:

> Here an individual may well find the pleasure highly fulfilling and completely satisfying at the moment and yet wish to have more (i.e., to *repeat* the pleasure) at some point in the future (not necessarily immediately). Certain salient sensual pleasures leap immediately to mind: the pleasures of sex, of eating fine meals and drinking fine wines, of listening to beautiful music, of seeing great art, and so forth.... Given the appropriate distribution of such pleasures, it seems that an endless life that included some (but perhaps not only) repeatable pleasures would *not* necessarily be boring or unattractive. (Fischer 1994, 263–4)

As Fischer goes on to point out, religious persons can experience not only repeatable pleasures of the sort just mentioned but also repeatable pleasures that come with the repeatable activities of worship of and thanks to God. Thanking God for the repeatable (and unrepeatable) pleasures that He has granted is itself a source of additional pleasure.

Consider, now, the second alternative, which is that an individual's future goals, projects, values, and interests must be suitably related to his present goals, projects, values, and interests so that the former will now (in the present) be attractive to him. If they are not presently attractive, then he will now fail to find them sufficiently interesting and will not desire to have them as his own in the future. Without such an interest, nonexistence will seem preferable to immortality. In response to this horn of the dilemma, Fischer writes that

> it seems that an individual could value such an [unending] existence if he or she felt that the change in character would result from *certain sorts of sequences*…. Surely in our ordinary, finite lives we envisage certain changes in our values and preferences over time. For example, one may currently value excitement and challenge; thus, one might wish to live in an urban area with many career and avocational opportunities (but with lousy weather and a high crime rate). Still, one might envisage a time in the future when one will be older and will prefer warm weather, serenity and security…. Thus, there are quite ordinary cases in our finite lives in which we envisage changes in our characters— our values and preferences—and which are not so unattractive as to render death preferable. Why, then, could not the same be true of immortal existence? (Fischer 1994, 267–8)

What Fischer says is surely correct, but it is important to note that Christians (and, I will assume, at least some Jews and Muslims) actually expect a significant positive *change or discontinuity* concerning moral character in the heavenly afterlife that will not render unending existence unattractive. Indeed, if such a change did not occur, something would be amiss and perfect happiness would be impossible. However, the main point is this: If it is true, as I am assuming, that what each of us most fundamentally desires is to experience pleasure, then so long as this desire persists, it is not necessary to have a stability of nonmoral interests and purposes whose satisfaction is a source of pleasure. Indeed, the pleasure that satisfies this most fundamental desire might come from what are at present unimaginable, radically different interests and purposes. Moreover, contrary to what Williams says, this potential difference between present and future interests and purposes does not pose a problem for desiring the survival of death. This is because, at bottom, what is necessary to make postmortem existence attractive is that one's life be perfectly happy, not that there be any continuity between present and future nonmoral interests and purposes.

Williams, then, provides no convincing reason to think that the idea of perfect happiness is unintelligible. However, other challenges to the concept are not hard to find. For example, Baggini argues that death, while perhaps not welcome, is nevertheless necessary. It is necessary because without its occurrence one has no reason to act in the present moment. According to Baggini,

> [a]n eternal life might turn out to be the most meaningless of all. What would be the point of doing anything today if you could just as easily do it tomorrow? As Albert Camus put it in *The Plague*, "The order of the world is shaped by death." The very fact that one day life will end is what propels us to act at all…. Life must be finite to have meaning, and if finite life can have meaning, then this life can have meaning…. [L]ife's meaning has to be found in the living of life itself, and the promise of eventual death is necessary to make any action worthwhile at all. (Baggini 2004, 54–5)

Is Baggini right about the need for death to make action both possible and worthwhile and to provide life with meaning? There is good reason to believe that he is not. This is because what propels one to act is the fact that the ultimate goal of one's action, which is the experience of pleasure, is intrinsically *good*. We act because what is good is attractive and motivates us to act. Thus, Baggini is mistaken when he says elsewhere that "[m]oments of pleasure are precious *because* they pass, because we cannot make them last any longer than they do" (Baggini 2004, 133). Moments of pleasure are precious because they are intrinsically good and it is this intrinsic goodness that entails that they would be precious, even if they never passed.

In light of Baggini's argument for the supposed necessity of death for meaningful action, it is interesting to note that some have used the idea of an unending life to illustrate the perplexity created by the concept of the infinite. Consider the following thoughts of Erich Reck, which are cited by Fischer:

> Suppose, e.g. that every hundred years I have one bad day (for whatever reason). Then over the span of an infinite life (say a life that is omega days long—the smallest infinite), the number of bad days will still be infinite. In fact, the number of bad days overall will be the same as the number of good days (both omega). Or to modify the example a bit: suppose you have a bad day after ten days, then the next after 100 days, then the next after 1000 days; i.e., the intervals between bad days get longer and longer. Overall, there will still be infinitely many bad days, thus the same (infinite) number as the good days. Or to turn the example around: imagine that after ten days you have your first good day of your life, then the next good day after 100 days, then the next good day after 1000 days, etc. Overall you will still have the same (infinite) number of good and bad days. These kinds of examples are used in literature on the infinite to illustrate how different it is from the finite. (Fischer 2009, 159)

In light of Reck's musings about unending life, it is important to remember that bad days have no place in perfect happiness. Hence, the paradox of the number of bad days equaling the number of good days will never arise. Moreover, this paradox concerns an actual infinite. Perfect happiness, however, if it involves a continuous addition of days, will never amount to an actual infinite number of days. Rather, it will consist of an unending existence in which there will always be another day. Though it is certainly hard to get one's mind around this idea, the idea itself is not incoherent.

Another relatively straightforward objection to the view that life's meaning is to experience perfect happiness concedes the coherence of the concept of perfect happiness but asserts that one does not desire to be perfectly happy for its own sake. However, to claim that one does not desire to be happy for its own sake just seems implausible. For example, consider the following thoughts by the philosopher Kai Nielsen, who is no friend of the view of the meaning of life that I am presenting and defending in this book:

I shall, for a moment, as seems to me appropriate in this context, speak personally…. I do not feel terror when I dwell on death. Yet I know full well it must come and I firmly believe—believe without a shadow of a doubt—that it will mean my utter annihilation. Yet I am without such a dread of death, though, of course, when I think of it, I feel regret that I must die…. As I am now in possession of the normal powers of life, with things I want to do and experience, with pleasure in life and with people I very much care for and who care for me, I certainly do not want to die. I should very much like, in such a state, to go on living forever. (Nielsen 2000, 154)

Though Nielsen does not talk explicitly about perfect happiness, it is not uncharitable to take from his comments the concession that, were it possible, he would like to go on being perfectly happy without end. And why not? After all, it is hard to come up with any explanation for why one would want one's enjoyment of what is intrinsically good to cease. This is because the idea that one might desire either a perfect happiness that is limited in duration or an unending but imperfect happiness for its own sake is conceptually suspect, if not incoherent. Because desire is conceptually ultimately aimed at both the experience of what is intrinsically good and the avoidance of what is intrinsically evil, no person can either desire the cessation of perfect happiness or prefer the experience of an imperfect happiness over that which is perfect for its own sake. As the philosopher Thomas Talbott has written, "[i]t is simply not possible … not to desire supreme happiness for its own sake" (Talbott 2001, 423). Jerry Walls adds the following thoughts in support of this point:

Nothing short of [endless joy and satisfaction] will suffice to give us what we most deeply crave. The fact that we seek happiness is axiomatic…. Clearly, if some partial experience of happiness is desirable, perfect happiness is even more so. Either we have such happiness, or we do not. If we do not, then it is something we want, and if we never get it, our lives will end in some degree of frustration. On the other hand, if we have it, we would not want it to end. If it did end, then again, our lives would end in frustration. The only alternative to a frustrating end to our lives is perfect happiness, happiness without end. (Walls 2002, 195)

Given the difficulty of challenging the view that people possess a desire for perfect happiness for its own sake, someone might concede the existence of this desire but point out that its existence does not entail its satisfaction and, therefore, perfect happiness cannot be the meaning of life. Indeed, it might be argued that belief in the possibility of satisfying the desire for perfect happiness is no more than a conscious form of wish fulfillment. For example, Michael Shermer, the publisher of *Skeptic* magazine, writes that "[f]or human beings, it is much easier to suffer the slings and arrows of outrageous fortune when we believe that it is all part of a deeper, unfolding plan.... We want to feel that no matter how chaotic, oppressive or evil the world may be, all will be made right in the end" (Shermer 2011, C3). In Shermer's mind, the fact that it is easier to deal with the evils of life through the lens of a belief that we can end up perfectly happy is sufficient to discredit the belief itself. While the evils we experience are real, we know that perfect happiness will never be real simply on the basis of the fact that we desire it.

Three counterpoints warrant mention.

First, and most importantly, if the desire for perfect happiness exists and is not satisfied, then life is ultimately absurd.

Second, on what grounds does Shermer give the nod to or privilege what is evil in reality over what is good? In the words of C. S. Lewis, why should we "have no difficulty in regarding [our] emotion at the sight of human entrails as a revelation of reality and [our] emotions at the sight of happy children or fair weather as mere sentiment?" (Lewis 1970, 144) Contrary to what Shermer claims, might it not be the case that our attraction to a life story in which things end up well tells us something about the nature of reality? Lewis believes that this is the case. He recognizes that while the mere existence of a desire does not guarantee its satisfaction, its existence might guarantee the reality of the thing desired:

[W]e remain conscious of a desire which no natural happiness will satisfy. But is there any reason to suppose that reality offers any satisfaction to it? "Nor does being hungry prove that we have bread." But I think it may be urged that this misses the point. A man's physical hunger does not prove that man will get any bread; he may die of starvation on a raft in the Atlantic. But surely a man's hunger does prove that he comes of a race which repairs its body by eating and inhabits a world where eatable substances exist. In the same way, though I do not believe (I wish I did) that my desire for Paradise proves that I shall enjoy it, I think it a pretty good indication that such a thing exists and that some men will. (Lewis 2001a, 32–3)

Third, and in light of the second counterpoint, it is appropriate to mention that some individuals, for whatever reason, desire that God not exist. For example, consider the following comments of Thomas Nagel:

In speaking of the fear of religion ... I speak from experience, being strongly subject to this fear myself: I want atheism to be true and am made uneasy by the fact that some of the most intelligent and well-informed people I know are religious believers. It isn't just that I don't believe in God and, naturally, hope that I'm right in my belief. It's that I hope there is no God! I don't want there to be a God; I don't want the universe to be like that. (Nagel 1997, 130)

Now it seems only fair to point out that if the mere existence of the desire for perfect happiness does not entail that desire's satisfaction, then the desire that God not exist surely does not entail the nonexistence of God. Given that God's existence is necessary for satisfaction of the desire for perfect happiness (e.g. God must exist to keep persons in existence after death in order for them to experience perfect happiness), one cannot help but wonder what Nagel would say about the desire for perfect happiness. Given his desire that God not exist, does he also not have a desire for perfect happiness for its own sake? Whatever the answers to these questions are, there are other challenges to the idea of perfect happiness to address.

Perfect happiness: setting the bar too high

As I pointed out in Chapter 1, Augustine made light of the idea that perfect happiness could be found in this life because of the pain and suffering to which each of us, to one degree or another, is subject. Given that perfect happiness cannot be had in this life, the philosopher Kurt Baier states that a problem for someone trying to discover life's meaning "is to find a purpose grand and noble enough to explain and justify the great amount of undeserved suffering in this world" (Baier 2000, 122). Now if the experience of perfect happiness is the greatest possible good for an individual, then it would seem that, if any good is good enough to justify the great amount of undeserved suffering that a person experiences in this life, it is this good. Whether or not the possibility of experiencing this good provides an adequate explanation for the experience of undeserved evil in this world is the subject matter of Chapter 5. What is interesting to note at this juncture is that Baier insists that the idea of perfect happiness is actually too high a standard to be used for evaluating the quality of an individual's life in this world:

> The Christian evaluation of earthly lives is misguided because it adopts a quite unjustifiably high standard. Christianity singles out the major shortcomings of our earthly existence: there is not enough happiness; there is too much suffering; the good and bad points are quite unequally and unfairly distributed; the underprivileged and underendowed do not get adequate compensation; it lasts only a short time. It then quite accurately depicts the perfect or ideal life as that which does not have any of these shortcomings. Its next step is to promise the believer that he will be able to enjoy this perfect life later on. And then it adopts as its standard of judgment the perfect life, dismissing as inadequate anything that falls short of it....
>
> This procedure is as illegitimate as if I were to refuse to call anything tall unless it is infinitely tall, or anything beautiful unless it is perfectly flawless, or anyone strong unless he is omnipotent. Even if it were true that there is available to us an after-life which is flawless and perfect, it would still not be legitimate to judge earthly lives by this standard. (Baier 2000, 127)

In response to Baier, it is important to point out that, in "adopting" the experience of perfect happiness as the purpose of life, one is not making a choice of any kind, let alone an arbitrary choice (one made for no purpose whatsoever). One is simply recognizing perfect happiness for what it is, namely, a great intrinsic good. I have already pointed out in discussing Euthyphro's Dilemma in Chapter 1 that the goodness of perfect happiness is not a matter of what anyone commands, says, or chooses.

As to whether perfect happiness is a legitimate standard for judging the goodness of this life, it seems that Baier is trying to have it both ways. On the one hand, he seems to assume this standard himself when he raises the problem of evil and claims that there is no purpose that is good enough to justify God's permitting the amount of undeserved suffering (evil) that is present in this world. Presumably, Baier believes that had our earthly existence been thoroughly pleasurable and free of pain and suffering (perfectly happy), then there would not have been a problem of evil. That quality of existence would have been good enough to preclude any such problem. On the other hand, when someone else makes use of this standard to judge the quality of our earthly lives, Baier asserts that that person is guilty of setting the bar too high. If Baier's position is coherent, then it seems to follow that no one other than he (or someone who shares his view) is permitted to use the standard of perfect happiness either to assess or to justify the human condition. One can only wonder why he merits this privilege.

In light of Baier's argument, the following summary of the facts about perfect happiness is apropos: No one makes a choice about whether or not perfect happiness is good. It just is good because it is intrinsically so. Moreover, it is the experience of the goodness of happiness in this life, imperfect as it is, which in part explains our yearning for that happiness which is perfect. And the happiness that is perfect is certainly not too high of a standard in light of which to assess what meaningfulness, if any, might be found in this or any other life.

If this life is the only one that there is and our desire for perfect happiness cannot be fulfilled in it, then whatever the degree of meaningfulness that might be found in this life, its achievement will not eliminate the ultimate meaninglessness that comes from the inability to satisfy the desire for perfect happiness. Though he does not deny this point, Nielsen seems to believe that it is really insignificant because of the distinction between a purpose *of* life and a purpose *in* life:

> [I]f there is [no] God ... there is no purpose to life.... Yet, from the fact, if it is a fact, that there is no purpose to life or no purpose for which we are made, it does not at all follow that

there are no purposes *in* life that are worth achieving, doing or having, so that life in reality must be just one damn thing after another that finally senselessly terminates in death. "Purpose of life" is ambiguous: in talking of it we can, on the one hand, be talking of "purpose of life," or, on the other, of "purposes in life" in the sense of plans we form, ends we seek, etc. that result from our deliberate and intentional acts and our desires, including our reflective desires. The former require something like a god or a *Logos*, but the latter most certainly do not. Yet it is only the latter that are plainly necessary to make life meaningful in the sense that there are in our lives and our environment things worthwhile doing, having or experiencing, things that bring joy, understanding, exhilaration or contentment to ourselves or to others. That we will not have these things forever does not make them worthless any more than the inevitability of death and the probability of decay robs them, or our lives generally, of their sense. In a Godless world, in which death is inevitable, our lives are not robbed of meaning. (Nielsen 2000, 157)

Now, it is correct to say along with Nielsen that our lives are not completely robbed of meaning, if we are able to act for and achieve purposes *in* this life. But this cannot be the whole story, for the following three reasons:

First, the fact that we can act for and achieve purposes in this life in no way eliminates the fact that, in a Godless world, our lives are senselessly terminated in irreversible death. This termination is senseless because we are never able to achieve the ultimate purpose for which we yearn and are, if God exists, created, which is the experience of perfect happiness.

Second, some lives are far more meaningless in this life than others simply because of bad luck. Each of us is subject to some misfortune in this life through no fault of our own, but some are subject to far more than others. For them, there simply is not the opportunity to achieve an experience of the kinds of goods that are means to pleasure and to which Nielsen draws our attention. Hence, an implication of Nielsen's view is that life is ultimately deeply unfair, and an ultimately deeply unfair world is an ultimately deeply absurd world.

Third, we need to ask just what kinds of things, in Nielsen's words, are "worthwhile doing." Nielsen asks "can we not … live in accordance with ... the hope that we humans can attain a certain rationality and come to see things whole and in time make real, through our struggles, a truly human society without exploitation and degradation in which all human beings will flourish?" (Nielsen 2000, 158). Nielsen goes on to concede that this is a fantastical, Utopian dream, and surely it is. But what is also worth recognizing is that when we seek guidance from Nielsen about how to get meaning in life he encourages us to pursue moral or just behavior and suggests that this Utopian kind of behavior is *rational* in nature. However, as I argue in the next section, there is good reason to question whether such behavior in a world where our lives are senselessly terminated in irreversible death is overall or all-things-considered rational.

Nielsen draws our attention to the distinction between the meaning *of* life and meaning *in* life and argues that the failure to have the former does not entail the inability to have the latter. Baier is largely in agreement with Nielsen:

> There are ... two quite different senses of "purpose." ... In the first and basic sense, purpose is normally attributed only to persons or their behaviour as in "Did you have a purpose in leaving the ignition on?" In the second sense, purpose is normally attributed only to things, as in "What is the purpose of that gadget you installed in the workshop?" The two uses are intimately connected. We cannot attribute a purpose to a thing without implying that someone did something, in the doing of which he had some purpose, namely, to bring about the thing with the purpose. Of course, *his* purpose is not identical with *its* purpose. In hiring labourers and engineers and buying materials and a site for a factory and the like, the entrepreneur's purpose, let us say, is to manufacture cars, but the purpose of the cars is to serve as a means of transportation. (Baier 2000, 119)

I have already conceded to Nielsen that it is reasonable both to acknowledge the two senses of purpose and how they are related and to agree that our lives are filled with behavior that is purposeful in nature. However, Baier believes that the distinction between purposefulness as it applies to explaining behavior and purposefulness as it applies to explaining the existence of an artifact entails unpalatable consequences for a theistic view of the purpose of life:

To attribute to a human being a purpose in [the sense of the purpose of an artifact] is not neutral, let alone complimentary: it is offensive. It is degrading for a man to be regarded as merely serving a purpose. If, at a garden party, I ask a man in livery, "What is your purpose?" I am insulting him. I might as well have asked, "What are you *for*?" Such questions reduce him to the level of a gadget, a domestic animal, or perhaps a slave. I imply that *we* allot to *him* the tasks, the goals, the aims which he is to pursue; that *his* wishes and desires and aspirations and purposes are to count for little or nothing. (Baier 2000, 120; cf. Baggini 2004, 16–17)

Surely, however, Baier is overreaching here. While it is possible that a human being's having a purpose as an artifact is degrading for that human being, it need not be. It all depends upon what that purpose is. What if the purpose is that that person be perfectly happy? Is that offensive and degrading for that individual? It is hard to see how it is because it seems to be in the person's overall or long-term best interest. Does it entail that the individual's wishes, desires, aspirations, and purposes count for nothing? It is hard to see how that is the case, if one's wish and desire for perfect happiness can be satisfied.

Moreover, wishing for, desiring, and aspiring to perfect happiness hardly seems degrading. Perhaps Baier believes that it is degrading because the individual does not have any choice about what he or she ultimately wishes for, desires, and aspires to. A person is simply stuck with desiring perfect happiness and has no say about the matter. I suppose that if one believes that not having ultimate control over what one desires is degrading, then the theistic view of life's meaning does have a strike against it. But why would having such control be good? What would it make possible? Would one be free to choose to make perfect unhappiness the ultimate object of one's desire and the purpose for which one acts? Surely we have passed over into talking complete nonsense at this point. As I pointed out in Chapter 1, the assertion that one might choose and pursue that which is intrinsically evil or bad for its own sake is necessarily false because it is a conceptual truth that desire ultimately aims at experiencing what is intrinsically good and avoiding what is intrinsically evil. And if this is the case, then Baier's atheistic view of life also is degrading, because no one in an atheistic world, just as no one in a theistic world, has ultimate control over what is desired. Therefore, in the final analysis, Baier fails to make a convincing case for the view that a person's being an artifact is necessarily degrading.

"Why should I be moral?"

In the previous section, I briefly noted Nielsen's claim that moral action is rational action that provides meaning for persons whose existence is irreversibly terminated at death. Nielsen is not alone in espousing this view. Consider what the philosopher Bertrand Russell has to say about our world as depicted by science and how we should live in it:

> [P]urposeless [and] ... void of meaning ... is the world which science presents for our belief. Amid such a world, if anywhere, our ideals must find a home. That man is the product of causes which had no prevision of the end they were achieving; that his origin, his growth, his hopes and fears, his loves and his beliefs, are but the outcome of accidental collocations of atoms; that no fire, no heroism, no intensity of thought and feeling, can preserve an individual life beyond the grave; that all the labors of the ages, all the devotion, all the inspiration, all the noonday brightness of human genius, are destined to extinction in the vast death of the solar system, and that the whole temple of man's achievement must inevitably be buried beneath the debris of a universe in ruins—all these things, if not quite beyond dispute, are yet so nearly certain that no philosophy which rejects them can hope to stand. Only within the scaffolding of these truths, only in the firm foundation of unyielding despair, can the soul's habitation henceforth be safely built.
>
> Shall we worship force, or shall we worship goodness? ... The answer to this question is very momentous and affects profoundly our whole morality. The worship of force ... is the result of failure to maintain our own ideals against a hostile universe: it is itself a prostrate submission to evil.... Let us admit that, in the world we know, there are many things that would be better otherwise, and that the ideals to which we do and must adhere are not realized in the realm of matter. Let us preserve our

respect for truth, for beauty, for the ideal of perfection which life does not permit us to attain, though none of those things meets with the approval of the unconscious universe. If power is bad, as it seems to be, let us reject it from our hearts. In this lies man's true freedom: in determination to worship only the God created by our own love of the good, to respect only the heaven which inspires the insight of our best moments.... Let us learn, then, that energy of faith which enables us to live constantly in the vision of the good; and let us ascend, in action, into the world of fact, with that vision always before us.... To abandon the struggle for private happiness, to expel all eagerness of temporary desire, to burn with passion for eternal things—this is emancipation, and this is the free man's worship. (Russell 2000, 72–6)

As inhabitants of a world that, by hypothesis, has no concern whatsoever for our own good either as individuals or a group, Russell insists that each of us should abandon any struggle for his or her own happiness and instead burn with passion for things like truth, beauty, (moral) perfection, and, most generally, the good. But, one might ask, why should I concern myself with these things? After all, something like aiming for moral perfection can be costly for one's own well-being. Morality, if it is anything, is a matter of restraint and self-sacrifice. As Baier says, "To be moral is to refrain from doing to others what, if they followed reason, they would not do to themselves, and to do for others what, if they followed reason, they would want to have done" (Baier 2000, 129). So being moral is a matter of being reasonable. But is it all-things-considered or overall reasonable for one to exercise restraint and sacrifice one's own best interest (happiness), if this is the only life that one has to live and there is nothing after death? Given that this life is all that there is, might it not be just as overall rational to maximize one's own well-being as best as one can, even if that requires that one act immorally? The philosopher Walter T. Stace, who shares Russell's and Baier's view that there is no afterlife of any kind, says the following: "I remember a fellow student in my college days, an ardent Christian, who told me that if he did not believe in a future life, in heaven and hell, he would rape, murder, steal and be a drunkard. That is what I call being a sham civilized being" (Stace 2000, 92). What the student presumably was trying to express is the idea that it is hard, or at least not easy, to see the overriding rationality of being moral when one could better promote one's own good by being immoral, given that everyone is going to end up in the same *final* state of being dead, regardless of how he or she behaves. The writer Joy Davidman, who converted from atheism to Christianity and toward the end of her life married C. S. Lewis, wrote that, as an atheist, she "had rejected all morality as a pipe dream. If life had no meaning, what was there to live for except pleasure?" (Davidman 2009, 8) Elsewhere, she wrote that "one's whole approach to life, one's whole philosophy turns on this point. If this life is all, then our goal is simple—to enjoy it as much as possible and make it last as long as possible and any talk of 'social duty' is mere irrational sentimentality" (Davidman 2009, 127). The Apostle Paul expressed a similar point of view in his first letter to the Corinthians: "If the dead are not raised, 'Let us eat and drink, for tomorrow we die'" (First Letter of Paul to the Corinthians 15:32). In short, given that it is reasonable to promote one's own well-being and one can do this better by being immoral, being immoral is, at least in some situations, equally, if not more, rational than being moral.

In the rest of this chapter, I argue that being immoral (when it improves one's well-being) is overall as rational a course of action as being moral, if the world is as Russell describes it. Moreover, it is because being immoral sometimes pays, while being moral not only does not pay as well but also all too often is very costly for one's happiness, that our world, if it is as Russell describes it, is beset by a deep form of absurdity. This absurdity is revealed in the fact that there is no sense of "more reasonable" to which one can appeal to explain to someone why he or she should be moral, when being so is contrary to his or her best interest and no compensation is forthcoming in an afterlife. But in an ultimately meaningful world it is more reasonable to be moral because in the end morality and self-interest are reconciled and embrace. In making my argument, I draw heavily upon an article by the theist philosopher George Mavrodes entitled "Religion and the Queerness of Morality" (Mavrodes 1986). Mavrodes calls the world as described by Russell a "Russellian world." Part and parcel of a Russellian world is what Mavrodes terms "Russellian goods," which include such things as a good reputation, sexual pleasure, and contented old age, all of which further one's happiness. What is also part and parcel of a Russellian world are moral obligations that require one to act (or refrain from acting) in various ways. Mavrodes goes on to say that unless we are greatly mistaken about our obligations, it seems clear that in a Russellian world there are an appreciable number of cases in which fulfilling an obligation would result in a loss of good to ourselves. On the most prosaic level, this must be true of some cases of repaying a debt, keeping a promise, refraining from stealing, and so on. And it must also be true of those rarer but more striking cases of obligation to risk death or serious injury in the performance of a duty.... Pleasure, happiness, esteem, contentment, self-realization, knowledge—all of these can suffer from the fulfillment of a moral obligation. (Mavrodes 1986, 217)

In conclusion, says Mavrodes, a Russellian world includes

moral obligations whose fulfillment will result in a net loss of good to the one who fulfills them. I suggest, however, that it would be very strange to have such obligations—strange not simply in the sense of being unexpected or surprising but in some deeper way.... Perhaps the best thing to say is that were it a fact that we had such obligations, then the world that included such a fact would be absurd—we would be living in a crazy world. (Mavrodes 1986, 218)

According to Mavrodes, a world that is deeply meaningful is one in which being moral is ultimately in one's best interest. In terms of question (3) in Chapter 1, such a world is one in which things ultimately fit together in an intelligible way. A world that is Russellian in character is deeply absurd or meaningless because it gives rise to individuals who desire to be perfectly happy while being morally obligated to act in ways that result in the uncompensated loss of instrumental goods that would provide them with the pleasures and happiness that they desire. In short, a Russellian world is deeply absurd because it results in lives in which things do not fit together in an intelligible way. Given that there are no goods available in an afterlife to compensate for the loss of Russellian goods (and the happiness they provide) that results from being moral, one would have a more meaningful life (one would have a life with more pleasure in it, where this good satisfies to a greater degree one's desire for perfect happiness) if one were to act immorally on those occasions when one could get away with it. In terms of having a meaningful life, it is irrational to be moral when being moral will in the end leave one worse off in terms of Russellian goods and the happiness that they make possible. So, if being moral is ultimately contrary to one's best interest, why be moral?

There are several replies that might be given to Mavrodes' argument by those who believe our world is Russellian in nature. First, one can simply admit that Mavrodes is right and that a Russellian world is a crazy world. This is the position of John Kekes, who insists that "[i]mmoral ... lives could have sufficient satisfactions to make them meaningful" (Kekes 2008, 258). He points out that this "is hard to accept because it outrages our moral sensibility .... Accepting it, however, has the virtue of doing justice to the plain fact that many evil and morally unconcerned people live meaningful lives" (Kekes 2008, 258). I would only add that a world in which immoral lives are meaningful lives is hard to accept because it outrages our *reason* in the form of an understanding of how things should fit together in an intelligible way.

A second response to Mavrodes is that he is just wrong: for every moral obligation that one fulfills, one receives (is compensated by) in this world a corresponding Russellian benefit, so that, in the end, one is not worse off in terms of one's happiness. Mavrodes notes that while there is nothing contradictory about such a response, it is just false (Mavrodes 1986, 217). As an illustration of its falsity, consider whistle-blowers, people who blow the whistle on wrongdoing of which they are aware in the course of their employment. These individuals are regularly harassed by fellow workers, ostracized, fired, and find it difficult to obtain further employment and pay their bills (Polman 1989). For them, being moral results in a significant diminishment of Russellian goods and, thereby, happiness. John Kronen and Eric Reitan put the point succinctly: "many of the most virtuous suffer from wholly undeserved ... social persecution, and it would be very difficult ... to prove that the general experience of mankind shows that, in *this* life, vice breeds misery and virtue happiness" (Kronen and Reitan 2011, 185).

A third response to Mavrodes' argument concedes that some people who are moral frequently end up worse off in terms of Russellian goods and happiness. However, for all of these individuals this loss is more than made up for by the pleasure and inner sense of satisfaction that they derive from being moral (this does not imply that their motivation for being moral is to derive this satisfaction; after all, one wonders if they are even acting morally, if that is their motivation). So while they are less well off in terms of Russellian goods, they are happier in terms of their inner well-being that is improved by acting morally.

The major problem with this rebuttal is that, like the previous one, it is just false. While some people who are moral end up happier in terms of their inner well-being (and even in terms of their Russellian goods), others do not. Mother Teresa is an excellent example. In addition to sacrificing Russellian goods for the purpose of ministering to the downtrodden in Calcutta, she revealed in private letters (from which I quoted at the outset of this chapter) that she suffered from a prolonged inner darkness of the soul from which she never escaped. Mavrodes' point is that a Russellian world is deeply absurd in so far as it makes moral demands of us that are costly in terms of our happiness.

Someone might respond that Mother Teresa's behavior is not irrational in terms of morality in a Russellian world, because acting morally is by definition acting rationally. Mavrodes' point, however, is not that acting morally is not in itself a rational course of action. It is rather that a world that is deeply meaningful is one where the demands of morality are not only by definition rational, but also consistent with the equally reasonable demands of self-interest, so that those who act morally never end up worse off in terms of their own well-being. And a Russellian world is not this kind of world.

A slightly different formulation of this third response to Mavrodes does not appeal to the pleasure that accompanies being moral but to the pain that attends being immoral. This point is sometimes made in terms of the concept of conscience. For example, Darwin said the following:

At the moment of action, man will no doubt be apt to follow the stronger impulse; and though this may occasionally prompt him to the noblest deeds, it will far more commonly lead him to gratify his own desire at the expense of other men. But after their gratification, when past and weaker impressions are contrasted with the ever-enduring social instincts, retribution will surely come. Man will then feel dissatisfied with himself, and will resolve with more or less force to act differently for the future. This is conscience, for conscience looks backwards and judges past actions, inducing that kind of dissatisfaction which, if weak, we call regret, and if severe, remorse. (quoted in Midgley 2010, 57–8)

In terms of Mavrodes' argument, the point here is that people who act immorally, while they might end up better off in terms of Russellian goods and the initial pleasure they provide, end up worse off in the end because of the pain produced by conscience concerning their earlier misdeeds.

Once again we have a response whose problem is that it is just false. While conscience is certainly real and plays an important role in our lives (for more on this role, see Chapter 5), it can be silenced through fabricated excuses, self-delusion, anger, and repeated wrongdoing. There is what is known as a "seared conscience" and it is something that can come in handy in a Russellian world.

A fourth challenge to Mavrodes' claim that a Russellian world that contains moral obligations is deeply absurd is an argument that begins with the following premise:

(A) It is in everyone's best interest (including mine) for everyone (including me) to be moral.

In (A), "best interest" is to be understood as "Russellian best interest" (having Russellian goods). Why think that (A) is true? Presumably, one might support (A) by arguing that without morality, people will live in a state of nature where life is nasty, brutish, and short in the way envisioned by the political philosopher Thomas Hobbes. Let us assume, then, that (A) has some support. Given (A), one can next derive:

(B) It is in my best interest for everyone (including me) to be moral.

And from (B) one can derive:

(C) It is in my best interest for me to be moral.

And (C) answers the question "Why should I be moral?" and explains why being moral is not absurd in a Russellian world.

If we assume for the moment that (B) does follow from (A), there are still problems with the derivation of (C) from (B). As Mavrodes points out, what follows from (B) is not (C) but:

(C') It is in my best interest for me to be moral as long as everyone else is moral.

However, it is pretty obvious that not everyone else in this world is moral. Hence, it has not been established that it is in my best interest for me to be moral.

Mavrodes emphasizes, however, that, in addition to the problem of (C) not following from (B), there is the additional question of whether (B) follows from (A). Whether it does hinges upon how one understands the word "everyone" in (A). If "everyone" is read *collectively*, then (A) plausibly means:

(A') It is in *the group's* best interest for everyone (including me) to be moral.

The problem now is that though (A') is somewhat plausible, (B) does not follow from it because the group's best interest does not necessarily coincide with my best interest. After all, the best interest of the group might be furthered by my sacrificing my best interest. To take a well-worn example, I might be one of a group of seven individuals who need to fit into a lifeboat that holds only six people. All seven of us act morally by agreeing to draw straws, where the one who draws the shortest forfeits a place in the lifeboat. As things would have it, I draw the shortest straw. In this scenario, the group's best interest is furthered at the expense of my own best interest.

The other alternative is to read "everyone" in (A) *distributively*. When this is done, (A) plausibly means:

(A") It is in *each individual's* best interest (including my best interest) for everyone (including me) to be moral.

If (A) means (A"), then (B) does follow from (A"). The problem now is that (A") seems false. In a Russellian world, what is in my *best* interest is for everyone else to act morally while I act immorally (in as many situations where I can get away with it). Someone might respond, says Mavrodes, that if I act immorally, then so will other people (who do not already act immorally), perhaps reducing my benefits. John Kekes seems to have this objection in mind in the following:

It will be said ... that evil-doers may acknowledge that their well-being depends on general conformity to the required conventions, and still hold that particular violations, like their own, would not endanger their well-being. This, however, is not true. Even occasional violations threaten a society's general level of security and stability, and because of their threat everyone's well-being would be at risk, including the evil-doers' own. (Kekes 2008, 193)

Perhaps so, but it is also the case (as Mavrodes points out) that many other people already act immorally, regardless of what I do, so my acting immorally won't necessarily undermine my benefits any more than they are already undermined. On the contrary, it might very well increase my benefits. And, I would add, despots often spend decades living a lavish lifestyle that is built on the backs of the less powerful followers of convention.

A section not strictly necessary

The argument of the previous section is intended to support the position that morality's existence in a Russellian world is deeply absurd in light of the problem of morality and self-interest being at odds. One way to remove this absurdity is to abandon morality. However, many Russellians are reluctant to do this. They insist on the reality or objectivity of morality. For example, Kai Nielsen writes that

> [t]orturing human beings is vile; cruelty to human beings and animals is, morally speaking, unacceptable; and treating one's promises lightly or being careless about truth is wrong. If we know anything to be wrong we know these things to be wrong and they would be wrong and just as wrong in a Godless world and in a world in which personal annihilation is inevitable as in a world with God and in which there is eternal life. (Nielsen 2000, 155)

Given this reluctance to give up on morality, Russellians look for an explanation that will enable us to make sense of its existence. Not surprisingly, many of them turn to evolutionary theory and the idea of the survival of the species. In Mavrodes' words, they argue that "morality has survival value for a species such as ours because it makes possible continued cooperation and things of that sort. So it is no more absurd that people have moral obligations than it is absurd that they have opposable thumbs" (Mavrodes 1986, 219). Now the survival value of morality for the species is supposedly a function of the actions to which true moral beliefs give rise. As Mavrodes points out, however, while it is the case that beliefs lead to actions and thus are key components in the explanation of behavior (that by hypothesis has survival value), it is a mistake to think that beliefs must be true in order to produce that behavior. They could very well be false and still produce the same behavior. In this case, the truth of the beliefs is explanatorily superfluous. Thus, even if moral beliefs lead to actions that have survival value for the species, they could have that survival value without being true. Given that this is the case, there is no need for morality (moral beliefs that are true) in an evolutionary Russellian world because false beliefs about morality are sufficient for survival.

It is interesting to note at this juncture that there are atheistic evolutionists who agree with Mavrodes about the efficacy of false moral belief in explaining survival behavior. For example, the Russellian evolutionist Michael Ruse argues that the pressures of natural selection through the interaction of human genetics and culture have hardwired widely distributed dispositions to believe and act in certain ways into us. These dispositions have had adaptive value (they tend toward reproductive success and survival) and include ones that have given us a sense of moral obligation (beliefs about moral obligations). According to Ruse, moral beliefs exist not because they are true but because they are adaptive: "The Darwinian argues that morality simply does not work (from a biological perspective), unless we believe that it is objective. Darwinian theory shows that, in fact, morality is a function of (subjective) feelings; but it shows also that we have (and must have) the illusion of objectivity" (Ruse 1998, 253). In short, Ruse maintains that the belief in moral objectivity (that our moral beliefs are true) is a fiction that is useful for survival purposes. "In a sense, therefore, morality is a collective illusion foisted upon us by our genes" (Ruse 1998, 253).

Now, someone might insist in response to Mavrodes (and Ruse) that moral beliefs will promote survival only if they are true (there really are moral obligations). What might justify this response? The most plausible answer is that if there were no moral obligations, then people would cease to believe in the truth of morality and cease to act morally. The survival of the species would then be undermined. However, even if it is true that both moral behavior and survival would be undermined if people ceased to believe in the objectivity of morality, Mavrodes' point is that belief in morality's objectivity does not require its objectivity. Someone might now ask, "But why think morality is not objective, given that so many people believe that it is objective? After all, is not the fact that so many people believe it is objective evidence for its objectivity?" Mavrodes' point is that there is no reason to think that morality is objective in an evolutionary Russellian world, even though so many people believe that it is, because its objectivity has no survival value. It has no survival value because its objectivity does no explanatory work to promote survival. The belief that it is objective does this explanatory work.

What must not go overlooked at this point, however, is the fact that even if our beliefs about morality are, for whatever reason, both true and have survival value for the species, this in no way undermines Mavrodes' central claim that morality in a Russellian world is absurd because it all too often leads to an irreversible reduction in Russellian goods and happiness *for the individual* who is moral. The question "Why (in a Russellian world) should I be moral for the sake of the good of other individuals or even the species when being moral decreases my share of Russellian goods?" is a question with no good answer. Therefore, life is fundamentally absurd in a world where self-interest and morality never ultimately meet to kiss and embrace.

In a further effort to rebut Mavrodes' argument, some might insist that he has misunderstood evolutionary theory: rather than morality having survival value for the species, it enhances the survival of an individual's genes. In general terms, the idea is that the restraint and cooperation dictated by morality helps promote the likelihood that a person (or his or her closest genetic relations) will survive to reproduce and pass on his or her genes. And to succeed at passing on one's genes is in one's best interest and a Russellian benefit.

This line of reasoning is no more successful in eliminating the absurdity of morality in a Russellian world than that which appeals to the survival value of morality for the species. For example, the distinction between belief and feelings about morality and objective morality itself comes into play once again in undermining the idea that it is objective morality that has survival value. Moreover, even if our moral beliefs are true, this new line of reasoning does not falsify the position that in at least some cases being moral leads to a reduction in Russellian goods and happiness for the individual who is moral. Given that this is the case, what overriding reason does this person have for being moral? Ruse, who believes the essence of the evolutionary account is about genes and not the species, says he would not "have those of us who see the illusory nature of morality's objectivity [jettison] moral thought.... Why should we forego morality ...?" (Ruse 1998, 253). Well, a reason for foregoing morality in a Russellian world (which is the nature of our world, according to Ruse), when one can get away with doing so, is that one can enlarge one's share of Russellian goods and make a more meaningful life for oneself. Ruse adds that "[i]n the case of morality, we are all part of the game, and even those of us who realize this have no desire to drop out" (Ruse 1998, 257). Maybe Ruse has no desire to drop out, but he is silent when it comes to explaining why someone who does not share his desire to remain in the game should not drop out, when he or she can do so without suffering any or minimal ill effects and, thereby, create a more meaningful life for himself or herself. Ruse does state that "we all have moral sentiments and simply breaking with them would cause great internal tensions" (Ruse 1998, 271). For some people, this is surely the case. But for others it is just as surely not the case. And it is for the latter that, on at least some occasions, not dropping out seems impossible to justify from the perspective of a meaningful life in a Russellian world.

"Why should I be moral?" again

If the reasoning set forth in the two previous sections is correct, it is hard to make sense out of morality in a Russellian world, a world in which psychological phenomena like experiences of pleasure and pain and the capacities to think and choose are *surface* features that mysteriously arise relatively late on the scene of our planet's history out of what was purely nonpsychological in nature. As Russell says, "a strange mystery it is" (Russell 2000, 72) that an accidental collocation of atoms eventually brought forth beings, such as ourselves, with *deep* moral obligations, obligations that ought to be kept even though the reality that gave rise to them is not committed to making sure that those who keep them will end up better off for having done so. Morality in such a world seems deeply absurd because it results in lives that are deeply absurd. Though this is how things seem, the atheist philosopher William Sinnott-Armstrong has recently attempted to defend the view that it is reasonable to be moral in a Russellian world. For starters, Sinnott-Armstrong says that

> despite popular rumors, it is normally in our interest to be moral. Immorality rarely pays. Sure, some people get away with horrible misbehavior, but the odds are against them. When people cheat, steal, or kill, they take big chances. And even if they can get away with it, they usually won't be happier, or much happier, than if they had made more modest gains honestly. They will often be hounded by guilt or fear of rivals or of punishment.... Thus, even if our only reasons were based on self-interest, we would still almost always have strong reasons to be moral. (Sinnott-Armstrong 2009, 113–14)

Sinnott-Armstrong claims that immorality rarely pays. The truth is that it often pays. Maybe horrible misbehavior rarely pays, but that truth, if it is a truth (again, evidence to the contrary is that despots all over the world and down through the ages have lived in luxury at the expense of their less fortunate subjects), does nothing to undermine the truth that nonhorrible misbehavior (e.g. petty theft and fraud) often pays. And while it is surely the case that some who are immoral are hounded by guilt and are less happy than they would be if they had acted uprightly, there are those who are not ridden by guilt but are quite happy because of what they have obtained through immoral means. Nothing that Sinnott-Armstrong says in the quote above negates these facts. Furthermore, nothing that Sinnott-Armstrong says addresses the question about the absurdity of morality in a Russellian world. Mavrodes would surely point out to Sinnott-Armstrong that, in a Russellian world, those who act immorally with impunity and are happier overall for doing so are being more reasonable in terms of their self-interest than they would have been had they acted morally. In their lives, immorality and self-interest go hand in hand and this makes for a deeply absurd world. Though morality presents its own rational demands to us, there is no convincing explanation for why these demands should trump the reasonable demands of self-interest, when the latter can be better promoted through immoral action. Moreover, given a Russellian world, those who choose not to act immorally because they would be hounded by guilt and fear for doing so might (as I have already pointed out two sections back in responding to Darwin's comments about conscience) try to rid themselves of such psychological hang-ups. Were their attempt to succeed, they might procure more Russellian goods and be much happier.

In light of the foregoing reasoning, Sinnott-Armstrong admits that harming others is sometimes in some people's best interest, even considering probable costs, and he asks whether this implies that these people have no reason at all to be moral. He answers, "No," and says "[t]hat conclusion would follow only if every reason had to be self-interested, selfish, or egoistic. There is [however] no basis for that assumption" (Sinnott-Armstrong 2009, 114). Indeed, says Sinnott-Armstrong, there are reasons for acting that are not based on self-interest, and moral reasons are such: "The fact that an act causes harm to others is a reason not to do that act, and the fact that an act prevents harm to others is a reason to do that act. There is, then, always a reason to be moral on this secular account. And often these reasons are adequate, because they are strong enough to make it rational (or not irrational) to be moral" (Sinnott-Armstrong 2009, 117). Nevertheless, continues Sinnott-Armstrong, even though there is a reason to be moral, not all will be moral:

[S]ome people still wish for a reason that is strong enough to motivate *everyone* to be moral and also to make it *always* irrational to be immoral. I doubt that secular moral theories can establish that strong kind of reason to be moral....
Is this limitation a problem for secular accounts of morality? I doubt that, too. If we demand this extreme kind of reason to be moral, then we are bound to be disappointed. The solution to our disappointment is to give up this demand, not to imagine a higher power that we want to fulfill an illegitimate demand. (Sinnott-Armstrong 2009, 118)

Mavrodes would likely (and rightly) point out to Sinnott-Armstrong that the problem he (Mavrodes) is raising is not that on a Russellian worldview it is difficult to find a moral reason that will motivate everyone to be moral. Rather, the problem is that our world, if it is Russellian in character, is deeply absurd because of its inclusion of some lives where moral behavior is ultimately counterproductive to self-interest and immoral behavior promotes self-interest. With respect to that problem, Sinnott-Armstrong simply concedes that the secularist (Russellian) account of morality cannot make it always rational in terms of self-interest to be moral. On some occasions, acting immorally is in a person's best interest and the secularist cannot explain why on such occasions it would be overall rational to act morally. Sinnott-Armstrong is well aware of how introduction of an afterlife and the existence of God changes things. The following is his summary of a theistic line of reasoning:

> The problem with avoiding harm to others [acting morally] is that anything I do is finite. If I cheat a rival in order to get a job, he will be harmed unfairly, but how much does that matter? He and I are both going to die anyway. Indeed, our whole species will disappear by evolving into something else. And the Earth is going to be engulfed by the Sun in about four billion years. So a little harm now does not make any real difference to the big picture. It's nothing compared to eternity. And avoiding harm also doesn't matter. It's all meaningless. In contrast, God does make an infinite difference. So do eternal salvation and damnation. That is why only religion gives a truly meaningful reason to be moral, according to some theists. (Sinnott-Armstrong 2009, 127)

The following is Sinnott-Armstrong's response to this theistic position:

> The conflict is between those people who are satisfied to do what they can in the temporary world that they inhabit and other people who feel that morality and all of life are empty and ultimately meaningless unless they have some kind of eternal significance. These conditions can be called *finiphilia* and *infiniphilia*, respectively.... The conflict arises only because infiniphiles (or infiniphiliacs?) love the infinite so much that they deny that finite goods, harms, and lives have any meaning at all in the face of eternity.
>
> The problem with infiniphilia is that it robs us of any incentive to improve this finite world. Indeed, it gives us reason

to destroy this finite world if we need to do so in order to reach an eternal Heaven. Just think of suicide bombers. If this is the best that theism can do, then it cannot provide a sound reason to be moral. Nor can it provide meaning in this life. (Sinnott-Armstrong 2009, 127–8)

Sinnott-Armstrong's response, however, misses the mark. As I pointed out earlier, the infiniphilia (theist) need not maintain that finite lives with goods do not have any meaning at all. To the extent that people accomplish purposes in their lives that produce happiness for themselves, those lives have meaning. This is the case, whether the purposes are moral or immoral. And when being immoral better fulfills one's long-term best interest and one is not riddled with guilt and fear for being immoral, there is no explanation forthcoming from the likes of Sinnott-Armstrong as to why one should choose morality over self-interest. In the end, there is simply the insistence that one should act morally, or a complete ignoring of the issue altogether (cf. Bok 2010, 121; Churchland 2011). But as Mavrodes emphasizes, this matter warrants serious attention, and serious consideration of it yields the conclusion that a Russellian world is *ultimately* absurd because it includes lives in which being immoral is more productive of happiness for agents than being moral. In such a world, there is no explanation for why a person should be moral as opposed to immoral, when being immoral would better promote that individual's self-interest. In an ultimately meaningful world, acting morally should be a necessary condition for the betterment of one's ultimate well-being, which is perfect happiness. However, what should be is not the case in a Russellian world and, therefore, a Russellian world is ultimately absurd because it includes lives that are absurd in virtue of the failure of morality and well-being to meet and embrace in the proper way.

Furthermore, Sinnott-Armstrong's assertion that infiniphilia robs us of any reason to improve this finite world and instead gives us a self-interested reason (that one get to heaven) to destroy it in the way that suicide bombers do is simply not true. As I will elaborate in Chapter 5, according to theism it is in one's best interest to choose to try to improve this finite world by acting morally because it is those who so choose who ultimately promote their long-term well-being. Thus, theism can do what secularism cannot, which is to provide a context in which morality and self-interest ultimately meet and embrace.

Mavrodes argues that morality and what makes life meaningful (vz. Russellian goods and, ultimately, happiness) come uncoupled in a Russellian world. The conceptual link between them is severed. Baggini believes that we live in a Russellian world and it is interesting to examine how some thoughts of his about a meaningful life connect with the problem raised by Mavrodes. According to Baggini, "life is worth living just as long as it is a good thing in itself. Such a life has meaning because it means something to us, it is valuable to those who have it. Many things can contribute to this: happiness, authenticity and self-expression, social and personal relationships, [and] concern for the welfare of others" (Baggini 2004, 170–1). But why would one include concern for the welfare of others as something that gives life meaning for oneself, when being immoral ultimately better promotes one's overall self-interest? Baggini states the problem as follows:

> [I]t might be argued that because my account depends upon our determining what makes life worth living *for us*, it has effectively cut morality adrift .... The reason for this is that I have defined ... a meaningful life as one that is meaningful or has value *for us*, and it is always possible that someone may choose a life which is meaningful *for her* but which is thoroughly immoral. (Baggini 2004, 176)

Baggini says that there are two possible responses to this concern. First, one might just affirm that meaning and morality are not linked (in a Russellian world). But, adds Baggini, this does not entail that it is good for a person to live a meaningful but immoral life, because "if morality is separate from meaning, there is nothing good or bad in itself about living a meaningful life" (Baggini 2004, 176). Hence, given the uncoupling of meaning and morality, there is nothing objectionable in terms of evaluative concepts like "good" and "bad" in saying that a "Gestapo officer can have a meaningful but immoral life" (Baggini 2004, 176). Second, one might affirm that meaning and morality are connected.

As Baggini sees the matter, it is not terribly important which alternative we pick, where the one we pick depends solely on whether we believe that morality and meaning are linked. If we believe that meaning and morality are not linked, then we should pick the first alternative and maintain "that there are no grounds for saying that there is anything good [or bad] about an immoral life which has meaning" (Baggini 2004, 177). But surely Baggini is mistaken at this point. If not all value is moral in nature, then there are grounds for saying that an immoral life that has meaning is good. That is, if there is a *nonmoral* (not to be confused with *immoral*) value in the form of pleasure's intrinsic goodness (see Chapter 1), then a person who immorally acquires Russellian goods that are sources of pleasure experiences what is intrinsically good and, thereby, has a meaningful life. Such a person is happy and immoral.

If we believe that meaning and morality are linked, then we pick the second of Baggini's two alternatives and it follows that "a life which seems of value to the person living it is nonetheless not meaningful if it is an immoral one" (Baggini 2004, 177). But once again, Baggini is mistaken. If meaningfulness is a function of maximizing pleasure and minimizing pain, then a person who manages to increase his or her pleasure (and decrease his or her pain) through immoral means manages to increase the meaningfulness in his or her life. One might avoid this problem by stipulating that a meaningful life has to be moral. But this strategy is thoroughly *ad hoc* in nature and contrary to what seems to be the case. Baggini says the following:

> I have argued that the only thing that can make life meaningful is the recognition that human life is worth living in itself. To recognize this is to recognize something that is true of all human (and perhaps some animal) life. This means accepting that each of us has an equal claim to the good things in life, and that making a person's life worse than it need be is a moral wrong. (Baggini 2004, 177)

While it might very well be true that each of us has an equal claim to the good things of life (a statement that seems at odds with Baggini's earlier claim that there is nothing that is good independent of morality), Baggini has said nothing to refute the view that the most meaningful life is one that is filled with what is nonmorally good and that, where possible, the rationally self-interested person will seek to maximize through immoral action his possession of Russellian goods (the good things of life that produce pleasure) at the expense of another individual's possession of those goods. Hence, Baggini has not provided us with a convincing reason to think anything other than that his insistence that a meaningful life must be moral is thoroughly *ad hoc* in nature.

Two final observations are apropos. First, Baggini suggests that those who believe in God and the afterlife do so because their religious teachings fail to provide knowledge of life's meaning during their time on this earth: "[According to religious believers] we need to believe in both a God and an afterlife, for only that sustains the hope that a meaning to life which is not spelled out by religious teachings will be revealed in due course by a deity that has our best interests at heart. To do this requires adopting a nonrational faith that is in many ways contrary to reason" (Baggini 2004, 56). However, Baggini's suggestion need not be taken seriously. Religious believers do not (or at least need not) believe in God and the afterlife for the purpose of coming to know (in the next life) the meaning of life. They know the meaning of life here and now. Belief in God and the afterlife is (at least in part) rooted in the insight that, in a rational universe, self-interest and morality cannot ultimately be at odds with each other. The two embrace in a rational universe and God and the afterlife are necessary for achieving this union.

Second, Baggini says that "life is worth living just as long as it is a good thing in itself" (Baggini 2004, 170). Strictly speaking, what this means is that life is worth living so long as it is intrinsically good. Life, however, is not intrinsically good. Neither is it intrinsically evil. It has no intrinsic value of any kind. What is the case is that life is worth living only if the person living it experiences what is intrinsically good. And this is what generates questions about the relationship between meaningfulness and morality, because if a meaningful life is defined in terms of possession of what is intrinsically good, then it does not take too much effort to understand that what is intrinsically good might be obtained in either moral or immoral ways. And the problem for the proponent of a Russellian view of the world is explaining why it is unreasonable to act immorally to procure Russellian goods when one can do so and suffer few or no adverse consequences.

As Baggini says, "we are used to thinking of meaning and morality in life as being linked" (Baggini 2004, 176). The question is what worldview preserves this linkage that we are accustomed to thinking exists. Following Mavrodes, I have argued at some length in this chapter that a Russellian view of the world fails to preserve this linkage. The responses to Mavrodes' line of reasoning have all been less than persuasive. However, perhaps Mavrodes is making a big to-do about nothing. According to the atheist Sam Harris, "[i]njustice makes its victims demonstrably less happy, and it could easily be argued that it tends to make its perpetrators less happy than they would be if they cared about the well-being of others" (Harris 2010, 80). Well, what is this easy argument? Unfortunately, Harris does not say. What he does provide is the following set of comments:

> I have no doubt that I am less good than I could be. Which is to say, I am not living in a way that truly maximizes the well-being of others.... I know that helping people who are starving is far more important than most of what I do. I also have no doubt that doing what is most important would give me more pleasure and emotional satisfaction than I get from most of what I do by way of seeking pleasure and emotional satisfaction. But this knowledge does not change me. I still want to do what I do for pleasure more than I want to help the starving. I strongly believe that I would be happier if I wanted to help the starving more—and I have no doubt that they would be happier if I spent more time and money helping them—but these beliefs are not sufficient to change me. I know that I would be happier and the world would be a (marginally) better place if I were different in these respects. I am, therefore, virtually certain that I am neither as moral, nor as happy, as I could be. (Harris 2010, 82–3)

Harris says that helping people who are starving is far more important than most of what he does. But important in what sense? And for whom? One would ordinarily think this help is morally important because it improves the well-being of the starving. It is at this point that Mavrodes would ask, "But why help the starving, if one can be happier and have more meaning in one's life by not helping them? Why does morality trump self-interest at this point?" Given what Harris says, it is not implausible to think that he would respond that he should help the starving because doing so would give him more pleasure, make him happier, and give his life more meaning. Though one might question how it is that self-sacrifice and the loss of Russellian goods that it entails seems all too conveniently to make Harris happier than he would be if he did not sacrifice those Russellian goods (the fact that Harris does not at present engage in such sacrifice might suggest that he really believes not sacrificing for the starving enables him to possess more Russellian goods and, thereby, be happier), let us grant to him that he accurately describes his situation. What about others who are different from him in this regard? What about those who would be made happier by not helping the starving but by stealing, lying, etc.? What would Harris say to them? That this is impossible? Surely at this point it is Harris, and not the religious person, who has lost touch with reality. As I write these words, Muammar al-Qaddafi's Libyan army is engaged in a brutal military campaign against his fellow Libyan citizens in an effort to preserve his power and the wealth and leisure that he has enjoyed for decades at the expense of others. What would Harris tell Qaddafi? That he really would have gotten more pleasure out of life and been happier, if he had given up his despotic rule? One cannot help but believe Qaddafi would find Harris' position highly amusing. After all, if the world really is Russellian in nature, Qaddafi would wonder why he should have sacrificed his well-being for the sake of being moral toward others.

Though Harris claims it can be easily argued that those who perpetrate injustice are made less happy than they would be if they cared about the well-being of others, he acknowledges on the last three pages of the text of his book that those who perpetrate injustice might be equally as happy as those whom they wrong:

> Perhaps there is no connection between being good and feeling good—and, therefore, no connection between moral behavior (as generally conceived) and subjective well-being. In this case, rapists, liars, and thieves would experience the same depth of happiness as the saints. This scenario stands the greatest chance of being true, while still seeming far-fetched. Neuroimaging work already suggests what has long been obvious through introspection: human cooperation is rewarding. However, if evil turned out to be as reliable a path to happiness as goodness is, my argument about the moral landscape would still stand, as would the likely utility of neuroscience for investigating it. It would no longer be an especially "moral" landscape; rather it would be a continuum of well-being, upon which saints and sinners would occupy equivalent peaks.

Worries of this kind seem to ignore some very obvious facts about human beings: we have all evolved from common ancestors and are, therefore, far more similar than we are different; brains and primary human emotions clearly transcend culture; and they are unquestionably influenced by states of the world (as anyone who has ever stubbed his toe can attest). No one, to my knowledge, believes that there is so much variance in the requisites of human well-being as to make the above concerns seem plausible. (Harris 2010, 189–90)

Harris is certainly right about this much: there is much similarity between human beings that transcends culture. Thus, because peoples across cultures desire Russellian goods that give them pleasure and make them happy, we find Qaddafis and Stalins, and petty thieves and liars, at all times and places. It is true that the Qaddafis and Stalins cooperate with others, but what of it? All this shows is that they and their cohorts are unjustly happy and lead meaningful lives at the expense of the less fortunate. And while petty thieves and liars know the goodness of friendship, it stretches credulity to the breaking point to believe that they simply could not on occasion act alone in bettering their well-being at the expense of others. Finally, Harris' seeming insistence that the unjust could never be happier than, though they might be as happy as, the just is so *ad hoc* in nature as to require no further comment.

In the end, one cannot help but believe that Harris understands the truth that if this world is not to be deeply absurd, then morality and self-interest must ultimately meet and embrace. Hence, he is intellectually driven to assert both that he really would be happier in a Russellian world by giving up Russellian goods and helping the needy, even if he does not do so at present, and that the happiness of the unjust, though it might equal that of the just, could never surpass it. In Chapter 5, I will explain how theism preserves the link between morality and self-interest that Harris seemingly wishes to preserve.

When all is said and done, it seems as if the existence of morality in a Russellian world is absurd. The atheist Erik J. Wielenberg agrees (Wielenberg 2005). However, he seeks to minimize the damage of such an admission by claiming that a theistic world is beset by an absurdity of a different kind. According to Wielenberg, one of the most admirable types of moral action is self-sacrifice that ends in death for the agent with no afterlife to follow. This kind of moral action is possible in a Russellian world but not in a theistic one. So the latter is beset by a kind of absurdity that the former is not. In Wielenberg's own words:

> If God does not exist, then the universe is absurd in virtue of being fundamentally unjust. On the other hand, if God does exist, then the universe is absurd in virtue of the fact that admirable sacrifice is impossible. It turns out that the universe must be absurd in some respect, and hence the idea that the universe cannot be absurd loses all plausibility. (Wielenberg 2005, 94)

What Wielenberg finds admirable about self-sacrifice that ends in death in a Russellian world is the fact that there is no good afterlife to redeem the sacrifice in this life. However, such self-sacrifice in a Russellian world is absurd and a theistic world is reasonable because the latter contains an afterlife in which that kind of self-sacrifice is redeemable. If Wielenberg's point is that nothing short of this absurd form of self-sacrifice is genuine self-sacrifice, then he has merely stipulated a sense of "self-sacrifice" that suits his own argumentative purposes. As "self-sacrifice" is normally understood, there is no good reason whatsoever to think that those who endure great hardships and losses for the sake of others in this life and who are compensated in the afterlife for those hardships and losses have not engaged in genuine self-sacrifice.

Is being moral the meaning of life?

In the previous section, I assumed that actions that promote the happiness that makes life meaningful or worth living can be at odds with the actions required by morality. Hence the question "Why be moral?" is appropriate, when one can best promote one's self-interest by being immoral. But what if my conception of what makes life meaningful is all wrong? What if being moral is what makes life meaningful? What if being moral is the meaning of life?

Though up to this point I have for the most part been critical of the views of Baggini, I believe that his responses to the suggestion that being moral is the meaning of life are correct and warrant summarizing here. Two of his points are as follows: (Baggini 2004, 65–8)

First, if the meaning of life is to be moral, then it is those who are acting morally who are experiencing meaningful lives. Those toward whom the moral activity is directed do not have their lives made more meaningful by the happiness that is produced by that activity. But this seems to get things backward. The point of moral activity is to promote the happiness of others, and this promotion is sought because it is believed that happiness is the meaning of life.

Second, if being moral is the meaning of life, then the more successful we are in making others happy, the less opportunity there is to have a meaningful life. As Baggini says, "if the process of helping others is itself our primary purpose, then we are left in the odd [absurd] position that were we to help others too well we would risk leaving life with no meaning at all. [Being moral], if successful, would defeat its own purpose" (Baggini 2004, 66).

Now this last point is not merely theoretical in nature, especially for theists, because they maintain that there will be no morality in the afterlife or heaven. For example, C. S. Lewis says the following about this matter:

All right, Christianity will do you good—a great deal more good than you ever wanted or expected. And the first bit of good it will do you is to hammer into your head ... the fact that what you have hitherto called "good"—all that about "leading a decent life" and "being kind"—isn't quite the magnificent and all-important affair you supposed. It will teach you that in fact you can't be "good" (not for twenty-four hours) on your own moral efforts. And then it will teach you that even if you were, you still wouldn't have achieved the purpose for which you were created. Mere morality is not the end of life. You were made for something quite different from that.... The people who keep on asking if they can't lead a decent life without Christ, don't know what life is about; if they did they would know that a "decent life" is mere machinery compared with the thing we men are really made for. Morality is indispensible: but the Divine Life, which gives itself to us and which calls us to be gods, intends for us something in which morality will be swallowed up. (Lewis 1970, 112)

[The moral realm] exists to be transcended.... [It is a] schoolmaster, as St. Paul says, to bring us to Christ. We must expect no more of

it than of a schoolmaster; we must allow it no less. I must say my
prayers to-day whether I feel devout or not; but that is only as I
must learn my grammar if I am ever to read the poets.

But the school-days, please God, are numbered. There is no
morality in Heaven. The angels never knew (from within) the
meaning of the word *ought*, and the blessed dead have long since
gladly forgotten it. (Lewis 1992, 115)

If being moral were the meaning of life, then life in a heaven without
moral activity would be meaningless. But this would be an odd
affirmation for a theist to make. Presumably, life in heaven is the
most meaningful life possible. Hence, it is easy to understand why
someone like Lewis affirms the views that he does. As I have already
pointed out, he asserts that pleasure is intrinsically good and that
the experience of perfect happiness is the purpose for which we
were created. It is perfect happiness that, in Lewis' words, will
swallow up morality. Other theists sometimes have problems with
these claims. It is to their concerns that I turn in the next chapter.

3

Perfect happiness and its theistic critics

The problem of pleasure

In the previous chapter, I examined atheistic objections to the view that perfect happiness is life's purpose. However, Christians and, I will assume, other theists also have their share of problems with this view, and while not all of these objections are Christian or theistic in character in the sense that only a Christian or theist could raise them, Christian theists (again, they are the ones with whom I am most familiar) are some of the most vocal proponents of them. Many of these objections are concerned with the claim that pleasure is intrinsically good (where this concern is perhaps fueled by the mistaken belief that a view like mine includes the additional thesis that pleasure is the only intrinsic good), which is the foundation of the view that the experience of perfect happiness is the purpose of life. Furthermore, some philosophers simply wonder about the intelligibility of the claim that pleasure is intrinsically good, regardless of its relationship to theism. In this chapter, then, I examine a wide range of objections that in one way or another concern the intrinsic goodness of pleasure.

Pleasure cannot be intrinsically good: religious concerns

As Terry Eagleton observes, "'What is the meaning of life?' is one of those rare questions in which almost every word is problematic. This includes even the first one, since for countless millions of people who are religious believers, the meaning of life is not a what but a Who" (Eagleton 2007, 33). For example, when we turn to certain Christian religious believers, they claim that our purpose or highest end in life is not to experience pleasure absent any pain, which is perfect happiness, but is, in the words of the *Westminster Shorter Catechism* authored by English theologians in the eighteenth century, "to glorify God, and fully to enjoy Him forever." In the minds of these Christians, glorifying God includes first and foremost actions like worshipping, praising, and thanking Him.

However, the obvious question at this juncture is "For what are we supposed to worship, praise, and thank God?" One eminently reasonable answer is that we are to worship, praise, and thank God for creating us for the purpose that we experience what is intrinsically good, where the fullness of that experience is perfect happiness. If this is so, then the correct response to those who raise the objection that the purpose of life is a Who and not a what is to continue to maintain that the ultimate purpose of our existence is the "what" of experiencing pleasure absent all pain, but also to point out that God will allow us to fulfill this ultimate purpose only if we finally embrace glorifying Him. This requirement for experiencing perfect happiness is thoroughly reasonable (morally appropriate or just) because it is God who has made it possible for us to experience our ultimate good. The authors of the *Westminster Shorter Catechism* implicitly recognized that the "what" of complete happiness, as I have defined it, is the meaning of life when they stated that we are to *enjoy* God fully. The enjoyment of God is the experience of pleasure that comes from worshipping, praising, and thanking Him as we ought, and this enjoyment itself glorifies Him because it brings attention to Him as the giver of such a great gift (cf. Piper 2011). And perhaps it should not go unsaid that the worshipping, praising, and thanking of God that is a source of pleasure for the worshipper is also a source of pleasure for God. A single act can be instrumentally good in a multiplicity of ways.

So much for the "Who-what" objection. Other Christians dis-
agree with the thesis that the experience of nothing but pleasure
(perfect happiness) is the purpose of life for a second reason.
According to them, the claim that this happiness is the end of life is
perversely selfish or self-centered in nature. For that reason alone it
is suspect and should be rejected.

Surely, however, concern about one's own well-being is
thoroughly reasonable. If there is a primary justification for thinking
that God is good, then it stands to reason that it is that each
one of us is created for the purpose that he or she ultimately
experience perfect happiness. Hence, God is concerned with a
person's ultimate well-being just as much as the individual rightly
is. C. S. Lewis puts this point as follows:

> If there lurks in most modern minds the notion that to desire
> our own good and earnestly to hope for the enjoyment of it is a
> bad thing, I submit that this notion ... is no part of the Christian
> faith. Indeed, if we consider the unblushing promises of reward
> and the staggering nature of the rewards promised in the Gospels,
> it would seem that Our Lord finds our desires not too strong,
> but too weak. We are half-hearted creatures, fooling about with
> drink and sex and ambition when infinite joy is offered us, like
> an ignorant child who wants to go on making mud pies in a
> slum because he cannot imagine what is meant by the offer of a
> holiday at the sea. (Lewis 2001a, 26)

Still, some remain unconvinced. In the words of the theologian
Keith Ward, God "shows us what the perfectly fulfilled human life
is like—and that may come as something of a surprise to those who
think that human fulfilment is just a matter of ... pleasure.... God
tells us that our real fulfilment lies in losing ourselves, in caring
much for the weak and the poor, and in caring little about wealth
and possessions" (Ward 1998, 24; cf. Mouw 1990, 35–7). But if
we are to care for the weak and the poor, then is it not because
their real fulfillment consists in experiencing happiness from having
the instrumental goods that are provided through that care and are
sources of pleasure? And if the real fulfillment of the poor and weak
consists in experiencing happiness, then surely the real fulfillment
of those who care for them consists in experiencing the same thing.
As Baggini points out, "How can a person claim both that everyone

ought to live a full life free from suffering *and* that in his own case
it is more important to help others than to live such a life?" (Baggini
2004, 67)

Like Ward, other theists find it difficult to disentangle the
purpose of life from the purpose of morality. For example, David
Baggett and Jerry Walls write the following about the emergence of
utilitarianism (a view that assumes that pleasure is the only intrinsic
good) in its contemporary form:

> This [emergence] happened first because confidence in the
> Aristotelian/theistic vision of a distinctly human end or purpose
> was shaken, only to be replaced by the goal of mere happiness,
> understood as a psychological state. This attempt to explicate the
> goal of ethics as mere happiness, particularly by the utilitarians,
> inevitably became vulnerable to numerous criticisms. The notion
> of a human telos is a much richer notion than mere happiness....
> (Baggett and Walls 2011, 184)

I have argued for a theistic vision of a distinctly human purpose
of life where perfect happiness is a purely psychological state that
consists of nothing but pleasure. Baggett and Walls say nothing in
their book about what is wrong with this view. What they do in
the quotation just cited is slide from talking about the purpose of
life to talking about the purpose of ethics. Such a move is suspect,
given that we must distinguish clearly between the person who acts
morally and the person who is the recipient of this moral action. As
I have already stressed, while moral action is performed for the sake
of the happiness of the recipient of that action, it is not performed
for the sake of the happiness of the agent of the action. Indeed, the
happiness of the latter individual might be better promoted by him
or her acting immorally. It is to this latter fact that I devoted a great
deal of attention in Chapter 2.

A third concern of some Christians is that the thesis that the purpose
of life is to experience perfect happiness either flows out of or produces
an idolatrous attitude toward pleasure. Surely, however, the assertion
that pleasure is intrinsically good need not flow from or produce this
attitude. As I briefly indicated in discussing the first objection in this
section, the experience of the intrinsic goodness of pleasure is central
to explaining what it is that evokes our worship and praise of God in
the first place. One is thankful to and worships God for providing the

gift of experiencing pleasure in this life and the life beyond, because to experience what is intrinsically good is a privilege.

Fourth, some Christians want to know where the Bible says that pleasure is intrinsically good. One must concede that there is no place where the Bible explicitly affirms either this or that perfect happiness is the purpose of life. But neither is there a place where it denies these things. In my opinion, the reason why the Bible (and, I would imagine, scriptures in other theistic traditions) says nothing at all about such matters is because it is not a philosophical text that was written to address them. Those who read the Bible looking for statements about the concepts of intrinsic and instrumental goodness and the purpose of life seriously misunderstand the purpose for which it was written. It is not a philosophical treatise that is concerned with addressing these and similar matters. Rather, it is concerned with issues (principally, I believe, membership in, and the destiny of, the people or nation of Israel, where Israel is supposed to be a moral light to other people in a world in need of redemption from evil) that *presuppose* a reader already has or can acquire knowledge of the intrinsic goodness of pleasure (and the intrinsic evilness of pain) and the purpose of life through reason alone.

It is only right at this juncture to point out that Christians are not the only ones who mistakenly assume that the Bible is concerned with stating the purpose of life and clarifying for us what is intrinsically good and evil. For example, Baggini, who is an atheist, seems to make the same assumption, and at various places even points out how unreasonable different biblical verses or texts are as statements of the purpose of life (Baggini 2004, 16–20, 45–9). He concludes that "[n]o Christian or Jew ... can provide an adequate answer to the question of why God created us by referring to their sacred texts" (Baggini 2004, 16). True enough. But why think that those texts were written for the purpose of providing such an answer?

Fifth, because some Christians immediately think of what is evil and/or sinful when they hear the word "pleasure," they believe pleasure cannot be intrinsically good. The young prince Joachim von Anhalt, to whom the protestant reformer Martin Luther wrote the following letter, seems to have held this view about pleasure:

It often occurs to me that, as your Grace leads a quiet life, melancholy and sad thoughts may be the cause of such indisposition; wherefore I advise your Grace, as a young man, to be merry, to ride, hunt, and keep good company, who can cheer your Grace in a godly and honorable way. For loneliness and sadness are simple poison and death, especially in a young man.... No one knows how it hurts a young man to avoid joy and cultivate solitude and melancholy.... Joy and good humor, in honor and seemliness, is the best medicine for a young man, yea for all men. I, who have hitherto spent my life in mourning and sadness, now seek and accept joy whenever I can find it. We now know, thank God, that we can be merry with a good conscience, and can use God's gifts with thankfulness, inasmuch as he has made them for us and is pleased to have us enjoy them.

If I have not hit the cause of your Grace's indisposition and have thereby done you a wrong, your Grace will kindly forgive my mistake. For truly I thought your Grace might be so foolish as to think it a sin to be merry, as I have often done and still do at times.... Your Grace should be joyful in all things, inwardly in Christ and outwardly in God's gifts; for he gives them to us that we may have pleasure in them and thank him for them. (Quoted in McMahon 2006, 165)

What people often do, and the young prince perhaps did, is confuse pleasure with immoral ways (e.g. drunkenness, gluttony, and debauchery) of experiencing it. However, as I stressed in Chapter 2, feeling good is not the same as acting badly. Pleasure is an intrinsic good that can be pursued in both just (permissible) and unjust (impermissible) ways. Indeed, no one would pursue it in unjust ways if it were not at least believed to be good. It is pleasure's believed goodness that leads people to act unjustly in order to have experiences of it.

The fact that the word "pleasure" often has an evil connotation might lead someone to assert that the view of the meaning of life that I am defending is *hedonistic* in nature. It is. However, I am *not* defending hedonism. Hedonism is the philosophical theory that maintains not only that pleasure is intrinsically good, but also that it is the *only* intrinsic good. As I have already indicated at various points in this and the previous chapter, I believe that there is at least one other intrinsic good, namely, justice, which I will discuss further in the course of addressing the problem of evil in Chapter 5.

Sixth, there are Christians who believe that to maintain that pleasure is intrinsically good conflicts with the holding that God is good. This belief, too, is mistaken. In thinking about the concepts of good and evil, one must always be careful to distinguish between intrinsic and instrumental kinds of good and evil. I have already explained in Chapters 1 and 2 that to assert that pleasure is good and pain is evil is to say that the one is good and the other is evil in a nonmoral sense. To affirm that the intrinsic goodness of pleasure and the intrinsic evilness of pain are nonmoral in nature is to say that their value is *not moral* in kind. It is not to claim that it is *immoral* or bad in nature, as when we say that a person is immoral. In contrast, God is good in a *moral* sense. God is morally good at least in part because He freely chose to create us for the purpose of our experiencing what is nonmorally, intrinsically good.

In spite of the distinction between nonmoral and moral goodness, some Christians insist that God is intrinsically good. It is plausible to think that they are confused about the distinction between the concept of being intrinsically good and that of not being able to act immorally. Being incapable of moral wrongdoing (to be necessarily morally good) is not, however, the same as being intrinsically good. The former is a moral value concept, while the latter is a nonmoral one.

The idea of being incapable of moral wrongdoing leads to a seventh concern, which is about the notion of God's sovereignty. As traditionally understood, God is sovereign in the sense that there are no "realities" other than Himself that exist independently of His creative activity. However, if pleasure is intrinsically good and pain is intrinsically evil independently of God's will/creative activity, then it seems to follow that God is not sovereign. God is not sovereign over but subject to these truths about pleasure and pain.

As I indicated in Chapter 1, when considering Euthyphro's Dilemma and C. S. Lewis' response to it, many theists like Lewis hold that God is subject to logic in the sense that He cannot do what is logically impossible. So, when it comes to truths like "pleasure is intrinsically good," it is plausible to insist that God is bound by it just as He is bound by the logical principle of noncontradiction (thus, God cannot at a some moment make himself both exist and not exist).

In this context, it is instructive to spend a moment considering how some Christian theists have sought to find a way through Euthyphro's Dilemma by arguing, for example, that moral rightness is a function of God's commands. Thus, William Lane Craig, following William Alston (Alston 2002), maintains that what is morally good is determined by the paradigm of God's just, loving, kind, and merciful moral character of which His moral commands, when He makes them, are not arbitrary but necessary expressions (Craig 2009, 30, 172–3). However, as Mark C. Murphy points out, if God's commands are purposeful in nature and serve as our standard of moral value in the way described by Craig, then God must have some prior notion of what constitutes a created person's prudential value or happiness. In Murphy's own words:

> For God to love us is for God to value us and want *our good*. For God to be kind to us is for God to act in ways that serve *our well-being*. For God to be generous toward us is for God to be abundantly gracious in bestowing upon us goods that make us *better-off*. The very virtues of God to which Craig wants to appeal to provide a grounding for moral value presuppose an independent and prior conception of prudential value.... What makes a state of affairs morally valuable (or disvaluable) is grounded in what makes people better- (or worse-) off. (For example, what makes the state of affairs *suffering's being relieved* morally good is that people are made better-off when their suffering is lessened; what makes the state of affairs *poverty's being on the increase* morally bad is that poverty tends to make people worse-off.) (Murphy 2009, 124)

Now, if I am right, while it might be true, as Craig maintains, that God's moral commands flow necessarily from his nature, the properties of that nature as described by Craig presuppose capacities whose exercise requires a concept of that which is to be produced in created persons for their good. In other words, a command of God's is an action that is performed for a reason. But a reason is a purpose or goal that God must have in mind and be seeking to achieve in giving a command. (In Chapter 4, I discuss at length the concept of purposeful explanation.) Most plausibly, God has the concept of perfect happiness for human persons in mind and this entails that He has in mind the concepts of pleasure and pain and of their respective intrinsic goodness and evilness. So, for God's commands to flow necessarily from His nature presupposes that He has knowledge of the necessary values of experiences of pleasure and pain and how those experiences are related to the happiness of a person. Or stated one other way, God's nature as depicted by Craig includes capacities for justice, kindness, love, and mercy that are essentially relational and logically presuppose or require the concept of that which is to be purposefully produced by their exercise. What I have argued throughout the first two chapters of this book entails that what is ultimately to be produced concerns experiences of pleasure without any experiences of pain.

But might it not be that "pleasure is intrinsically good" and "pain is intrinsically evil" are loving and merciful commands that necessarily flow from God's nature? The question now, however, is why does the command "pain is intrinsically evil" issue lovingly from God's character? Why does not "pain is intrinsically good" flow forth? The questions seem readily intelligible and appropriate. And ultimately the only plausible answer to them is that the command "pain is intrinsically good" would be less than loving and kind because pain is intrinsically evil, regardless of what anyone commands.

At this point, it is relevant to point out that Craig himself finds it hard to avoid recognition of the basic explanatory role of the concept of happiness. Indeed, he uses this concept (his favored expression is "prudential value") in an argument that is reminiscent of Mavrodes' about the absurdity of morality in a Russellian world (see Chapter 2). For example, Craig says that, on atheism, moral value and prudential value (one's own happiness)

> fall apart and are often in head-on collision. Acting morally will then not make prudential sense.... One has moral value pulling in one direction and prudential value tugging in the opposite and no way to decide rationally which choice to make. By contrast, on classical theism moral value and prudential value may seem temporarily out of joint but are ultimately harmonious, so that adopting the moral point of view makes good prudential sense, even if it involves worldly sacrifice.... If some action involves permanent, net loss to a person, then it does not make sense, prudentially speaking, to engage in it. Since on atheism, altruistic actions fall under such a description, they do not [ultimately] make sense. (Craig 2009, 182–3)

What Craig's reasoning confirms is that any plausible form of theism must take at face value the seemingly fundamental place that prudential value occupies in our everyday view of the world and incorporate it into a worldview in which it is ultimately harmonized with the demands of morality. Theism loses its intellectual "punch" if it does not accord prudential value the fundamental place that it seems to occupy. And as I have just argued, it is difficult to make any sense of Craig's claim that God's commands flow from His nature that does not require that God have a concept of a human person's optimal prudential value, which is perfect happiness.

With the work of William Alston as his guide, Mark Linville has also sought to answer Euthyphro's Dilemma in terms of God's nature (Linville forthcoming). Thus, in answer to the question "In virtue of what is God said to be good?" Alston's answer, according to Linville, is "God is good by virtue of being loving, just, merciful, etc." But, says Linville, one might ask "By virtue of what are these features of God good-making features?" And the Alstonian answer to this question is "By virtue of being features of God":

> On Alston's view, God's nature is the first principle of value, and we beg the question against his view if we insist that God and his nature must themselves be held up to some independent standard before we can meaningfully determine whether God is good. And as we have seen, any such standard faces the same difficulty, if indeed there is anything difficult.... Alston observes [that] ... "Sooner or later either a general principle or an individual paradigm is cited. Whichever it is, that is the end of the line.... On both views, something is taken as ultimate, behind which we cannot go, in the sense of finding some explanation of the fact that it is constitutive of goodness." (Linville forthcoming)

Now Linville (and Alston) are surely correct: sooner or later one reaches the end of the line. The question is whether one reaches it with properties of being loving, just, merciful, etc. The question "By virtue of what are these features of God good-making features?" seems to have an answer: These are good-making features insofar as they give rise to actions that have an effect on (a relational concept) people's experiences of pleasure (and pain), where the intrinsic goodness of pleasure is the first principle of value (and nonrelational in nature). In contrast, the question "By virtue of what is pleasure good?" seems not to have an answer. It is just good, period. In terms of what has value, it is the end of the line.

An eighth objection that is raised by some Christian theists concerns what St Paul wrote in his First Letter to the Corinthians 2:9: "no eye has seen, nor ear heard, nor the heart of man conceived, what God has prepared for those who love him." If this is true, then is it not the height of arrogance and absolute foolishness on my part to think that I know that nothing but pleasure is in store for us in the afterlife with God? Might it not be the case that pleasure is not the ultimate intrinsic good that we can experience but is like a sign along a highway that points us to our ultimate destination whose character is substantially different from anything that we experience in this life? In other words, perhaps pleasure is not the genuine article but a mere imitation.

Perhaps, but I doubt it. As far as I am aware, no biblical writer says anything philosophically detailed about the nature of heaven (as I have already pointed out in this chapter, the Bible is not a philosophical text). Maybe what St Paul is pointing out in his comment to the Corinthians is not that heaven involves some other intrinsic good than pleasure, but that we cannot at present comprehend the sources of pleasure in the afterlife. I would not even pretend to comprehend much about the nature of God, but if it is true that I am created to be perfectly happy, then it is plausible to hold that He will be the ultimate source of the enjoyment of what is intrinsically good in the afterlife. In the end, then, the following position seems reasonable: heaven won't be anything qualitatively worse than the experience of nothing but pleasure. If heaven does involve or consist of a greater intrinsic good than pleasure (again, I can see no reason to believe this), then so much the better for those who go there. What is the case, then, is that pleasure is not only intrinsically good but also our best approximation, if it is no more than an approximation, to what the experiential character of heaven is like.

Finally, certain persons, including various Christians, concede that pleasure is sometimes good, but go on to add that it is not always so. In their estimation, in those cases where it is good, it is an *accompaniment* of actions that are themselves good and it *perfects* or *completes* those actions in light of its own goodness. Because pleasure also accompanies immoral actions, however, and the desire for it leads people to perform them, it is wrong to think that it is intrinsically good and the experience of it alone is the purpose of life. What is intrinsically good cannot lead people to do what is wrong. Not all pleasure, therefore, is good. Rather, there are good and evil pleasures.

To illustrate their point, these persons sometimes use the example of sex. According to them, the purpose of sex between a man and a woman is procreation. The purpose cannot be the experience of the pleasure that accompanies the act of sexual intercourse, because that pleasure often leads to illicit sexual activity, unwanted children, single parent families, poverty, and abortion. Pleasure, therefore, cannot provide the basis for distinguishing between moral (permissible) and immoral (impermissible) kinds of sex or any other type of action. Rather, the distinction between moral and immoral action must serve as the basis for distinguishing between good and bad (evil) pleasures.

In order to formulate a plausible answer to this objection, it is necessary to keep clear the distinction between one's own purpose (which is to experience nothing except pleasure) and the purpose of the human reproductive system (which, according to the objector, is the generation of offspring). Because pleasure accompanies the sexual act, one and the same act of sex can be a means to trying to accomplish both purposes. On some occasions, however, justly trying to accomplish one of these purposes (the experience of pleasure) may not be possible because a necessary condition for justly trying to accomplish the other (the generation of offspring) is lacking. For example, while one can obtain pleasure from sexual intercourse outside of marriage, the mutual long-term commitment that is necessary to nurture and raise a child that might be conceived through that intercourse is absent. Therefore, one is morally obligated to refrain from sexual intercourse outside marriage and, thereby, is prevented from satisfying one's desire for the pleasure that accompanies the sexual act, even though the pleasure that would be experienced from such intercourse is intrinsically good. In short, the expression "bad pleasures" is, as Lewis stated, a kind of shorthand. By it we mean "'pleasures snatched by unlawful acts.' It is the stealing of the apple that is bad, not the sweetness. The sweetness is still a beam from the glory. That does not palliate the stealing. It makes it worse. There is sacrilege in the theft. We have abused a holy thing" and ignored "the smell of Deity that hangs about it" (Lewis 1992, 89, 90). Elsewhere, Lewis said "I think *all* pleasure simply good: what we call bad pleasures are pleasures produced by action, or inactions, which break the moral law, and it is those actions or inactions which are bad, not the pleasures" (Lewis 2004, 462–3). And again he wrote, "I have no doubt at all that pleasure in itself is a good and pain in itself an evil; if not, then the whole Christian tradition about heaven and hell and the passion of our Lord seems to have no meaning. Pleasure, then, is good; a 'sinful' pleasure means a good offered and accepted, under conditions which involve a breach of the moral law" (Lewis 1967, 21). Finally, in *The Screwtape Letters*, Screwtape reminds his devilish nephew, Wormwood, that pleasure is the creation of God:

> Never forget that when we are dealing with any pleasure in its healthy and normal and satisfying form, we are, in a sense, on the Enemy's ground. I know we have won many a soul through pleasure. All the same, it is His invention, not ours. He made the pleasures: all our research so far has not enabled us to produce one. All we can do is to encourage the humans to take the pleasures which our Enemy has produced, at times, or in ways, or in degrees which He has forbidden. (Lewis 1961, 41–2)

Pleasure cannot be intrinsically good: philosophical concerns

I turn in this section to philosophical concerns about my claim that pleasure is intrinsically good. While the concerns are legitimate, they are more technical in nature and will be more difficult for the nonphilosopher to understand. Given that this is the case, the more general reader can skip this section without missing anything of substance concerning the central thesis of the book. Nevertheless, for the sake of the nonphilosopher who decides to read further in this section, I have tried hard to make the topics that I treat as accessible as possible.

It is not only Christians who have been concerned about and raised objections to the claim that pleasure is intrinsically good. Others have their own problems with the view. At the end of the last section, I quoted C. S. Lewis' statement that all pleasure is good and that what we term "bad pleasures" are pleasures produced by immoral *actions*. As an objection to Lewis' view, it might be pointed out that "bad" pleasures sometimes occur in us *without any activity on our part*. Examples include the pleasures of learning that one's obnoxious coworker has terminal cancer or that an innocent person whom one disliked was tortured to death.

There is no reason to think that Lewis would not have acknowledged that there are bad pleasures that occur in us without any activity on our part. Even in these cases, however, he would have insisted that there is no good reason to deny that the pleasures involved are intrinsically good. Lewis likely would have maintained, and rightly so, that the complex situation of experiencing intrinsically good pleasure at the expense of the innocent is a whole (sometimes termed an "organic unity"; see Chapter 5) that is bad or evil overall because of the relation among its parts. It is the combination of experiencing intrinsically good pleasure at the expense of the undeserved misfortune of others, even when this occurrence of pleasure occurs without beckoning, that is bad.

Though experiencing pleasure is itself something with respect to which we are essentially passive and that sometimes accompanies other events in our mental lives with respect to which we are also essentially passive (e.g. learning that one's obnoxious coworker has terminal cancer), it often occurs with actions that we perform. The fact that it accompanies our actions in this way leads some to hold that happiness itself consists of activity of a certain kind (see Taylor's discussion of the myth of Sisyphus in Chapter 1) along with its accompanying pleasure. The kind of activity that supposedly is a component of happiness is typically termed morally *virtuous* (as opposed to vicious) and includes things like benevolence, patience, courage, etc. These *virtues* are said to perfect (make perfect) the person who exemplifies them, much as the sharpness, grip, and weight of a knife or the fabric, color, and shape of a woman's dress perfects each of them. The main idea behind this understanding of happiness is that an individual person, like an individual knife or dress, is an entity with a purpose or function whose fulfillment requires possession of certain traits (virtues) that make the possessor a good member of the kind "human being." It is the exercising of these moral virtues (acting virtuously) that should be accompanied by pleasure.

While this understanding of happiness is historically influential (one of its first noteworthy proponents was Aristotle), it mistakenly identifies happiness, which is essentially passion (something that happens to a person; see Chapter 1), with action (something that a person does). Even if morally virtuous activity were always accompanied by pleasure (Aristotle held that moral virtue is developed by habit and might not initially be pleasurable), it would not follow that the activity itself would be a part of happiness. Happiness would still consist of the pleasure that accompanies the morally virtuous activity.

Sometimes philosophers (again following Aristotle) contrast moral virtue with intellectual virtue, where the latter is something like the fitting engagement of our capacity to know. Given intellectual virtue, these philosophers suggest that our happiness consists, at least in part, of the use of our intellect. For example, John Kronen and Eric Reitan write that "[o]ur intellectual faculties are so central to our nature that most philosophers since Aristotle have agreed that our happiness must involve these faculties functioning well. Hence, supreme happiness must involve these faculties functioning perfectly" (Kronen and Reitan 2011, 85). But even if we assume for the sake of discussion that happiness (perfect or otherwise) involves our intellectual faculties in the sense that the former requires the use of the latter, it does not follow that happiness consists, even in part, in the use of the intellect. Happiness consists in the pleasure that accompanies that use.

When I teach my course on the meaning of life, I have students read Robert Nozick's thought experiment about an experience machine. As I noted in Chapter 1, Nozick asks his readers to imagine a machine, the programming of which will provide them with uninterrupted pleasure for as long as they wish (which, upon reflection, readers come to realize is for eternity), if they connect to it. As Nozick points out, a person who is connected to the experience machine does not have to *do* anything. An individual who is hooked up to the machine never has to *act*; he or she simply experiences pleasure. What Nozick wants to know is whether a reasonable person would accept an offer to connect to the experience machine.

According to the philosopher Daniel Haybron, "most philosophers have rejected hedonism and other mental state accounts [of well-being], mainly because of experience machine-type worries" (Haybron 2008, 34). And it is true that, on a first encounter with the idea of the experience machine, most persons wrestle with the idea of connecting to it. On the one hand, they understandably find the thought of experiencing nothing but pleasure extremely attractive. On the other hand, they are puzzled by the severance of pleasure from action, because the connection between the two is so pervasive in their own lives. While some people actually try to sever this connection through artificial means, such as recreational drugs, they know all too well that when the pleasurable effects of the drugs cease, the connection between pleasure and action will be reestablished. Most importantly, these individuals discover that they will have to act to take more drugs to recapture their "high." Students in my meaning of life course often ask me whether I would connect to the experience machine, and I always respond "Sure." What I also point out, however, is that the example of the experience machine seductively breaks the link between action and pleasure that, I believe, the concept of justice requires. The idea here, which I will develop in some depth in Chapter 5, is that because pleasure is such a great good, and perfect happiness is the greatest good because it is an existence that consists of nothing but pleasure, only those who in terms of the present discussion are virtuous *deserve* to experience it.

In other words, while it is possible conceptually to pull apart pleasure and action for the sake of a thought experiment like the experience machine, justice is the attractive conceptual force that necessarily draws them back together so that only virtuous people ultimately justly experience pleasure in the form of perfect happiness. But this requirement of justice in no way transforms virtuous activity itself into a constituent of happiness. And while it is not conceptually problematic to think that heaven might logically be the ultimate experience machine (an existence in which God constantly infuses the virtuous with nothing but pleasure without any activity on their part), there is no reason to think that it must be so. The blessed in heaven might, and on the Christian view will, continue forever to perform actions that are always accompanied by pleasure and of which, therefore, they will never grow tired (see Chapter 2). Many of the actions that are the greatest source of pleasure for us are performed in the relational context of friendships with others, and as Charles Taliaferro says concerning the Christian view of life's meaning, "[o]ur ultimate fulfillment ... lies in the good, fruitful relations with fellow creatures and in relationship (union) with God" (Taliaferro 2009, 216; for a few more brief comments about this issue, see the Addendum to Chapter 5).

The next objection concerns a matter of word usage. Its proponents begin by pointing out that if an experience of pleasure exemplifies the simple and indefinable property of being good (a simple and indefinable property is one that is not composed out of or definable in terms of any other properties), then the sentence "Pleasure is good" implies that the word "good" is being used in an unrestricted, unqualified, unconditional, or absolute sense. Words, however, often have more than one use and because "good" has a restricted, qualified, conditioned, or relative use, these objectors argue that we should be suspicious of its absolute use. In its relative use, "good" is restricted to the role of modifying a noun as in "This is a good novel," "This is a good kitchen knife," and "She is a good human being." What is the case with this relative use of "good" is that we have at least a rough idea of the properties of a thing that make it a good thing or member of its kind. Thus, a good novel is one with the properties of having a good plot, being the appropriate length, having readable print, etc. A good kitchen knife is one that is light in weight, has a good grip, is not too short or too long, and most importantly is sharp. A good human being is one who is patient, kind, cooperative, etc. According to the critics, given this relative use of "good," where properties can be specified that ground or justify its attribution to a thing of a certain kind, one has reason to be suspicious of its nonrelative or unqualified use in "Pleasure is good."

What one wonders, however, is why both uses of "good" cannot be correct. As the saying goes, why couldn't this be a "both-and" instead of an "either-or"? Now whenever there are two things (in this case, two ways of using "good"), questions arise about how they are related. In the case of these two uses of "good," it is extremely plausible to think that the absolute use of "good" in "Pleasure is good" is more basic or fundamental than, and explains the existence of, the relative use. Thus, a good novel is good because the specified good-making properties provide its reader with pleasure. A good kitchen knife is one whose good-making properties enable its user to prepare food that will be a source of pleasure. And a good human being is one who has the good-making properties that ultimately enable him or her to promote experiences of pleasure in others. In other words, "good" in "a good novel," "a good kitchen knife," and "a good human being" refers to what in Chapter 1 was defined as an instrumental good.

A slightly more sophisticated version of the argument just examined against the unqualified, intrinsic goodness of pleasure is developed by the British philosopher Peter Geach (Geach 1956) in response to the claim made by another British philosopher G. E. Moore that "good" is like "yellow," insofar as each term refers to a simple, nonanalyzable property (Moore 1903, 7). Geach argues that nothing can be just plain good in the unqualified way expressed by "pleasure is good" because all good is good relative to a certain kind of object. Geach believes that we can see this is the case because "good" is unlike "yellow" in the following way: whereas "x is a yellow bird" breaks up into "x is a bird" and "x is yellow," "x is a good singer" does not break up into "x is a singer" and "x is good." Furthermore, from "x is a yellow bird" and "a bird is an animal," we readily infer "x is a yellow animal," but from "x is a good singer" and "a singer is a human being," we cannot infer "x is a good human being."

But consider the following: "x is a good psychological event" seems to break up into "x is a psychological event" and "x is good," and from "x is a good psychological event" and "a psychological event is an event in a soul," we can infer "x is a good event in a soul." Nothing seems amiss in either of these cases (let "x" be "an experience of pleasure") so that nothing seems amiss with either the claim that an experience of pleasure is good or the assertion that an experience of pleasure is good in an unqualified sense.

Opponents of the absolute use of "good" will, however, likely persist with their objections. Some will maintain that *all* good is relative good in the sense that what is *good for* something is relative to the kind of thing that it is, and something is *good for* that kind of thing insofar as it helps that thing to *flourish* or *do well* (cf. Kraut 2007). Thus, just as water, sunshine, and warm temperatures are *good for* a plant because they help it to grow tall, flower, and smell fragrant (all of which are aspects of its flourishing), so also pleasure is *good for* a human being because it (along with food, water, and a multitude of other things) helps a human being to flourish. Pleasure itself, however, is not intrinsically good and, therefore, the absolute use of "good" is mistaken.

However, why can it not be that, in the case of a human being, what is most fundamentally good for it is something (pleasure) that is good intrinsically? Pleasure's intrinsic goodness by itself is all the reason that is needed to explain why a person should experience it, and pleasure's intrinsic goodness makes it *good for* a person to experience because it constitutes that individual's well-being. Instrumental goods that are *good for* persons are properly understood in terms of pleasure's being good for them. Thus, if knowledge, music, and beauty are good for an individual, they are so only because they are instrumental to pleasure. When it is good for a person P1 to have X but not good for a person P2 to have X, this is because X is an instrumental good for P1 but not for P2. But pleasure's intrinsic goodness makes it good for anyone to have because it constitutes a person's well-being.

As I briefly discussed in Chapter 1, a human being is a complex entity that is composed of a body and a soul. Thus, something like food is instrumentally good for a human body because the health of that body is instrumentally good for the well-being of its soul, where the well-being of that soul is constituted by experiences of nothing but pleasure. What about a human body when it is considered independently of its relationship to a soul? Is anything good for it? Does it have a good of its own? In a loose sense, the answer to this question is surely "Yes." Things like food and water are good for it, because they are instrumental to its growth in stature and function. But are they really good *for it* in a strict sense? Here I believe the answer must surely be "No." Because a human body is not self-conscious and sentient, nothing can strictly speaking be good for it. There is no "I" there for which things could be good. It makes no difference to a human body itself that it is full in stature and functioning well. Thus, because in a strict sense a human body has no good of its own, at most it can be instrumentally good in relationship to a soul that strictly speaking has a good of its own. What is true of a human body in this case is also true of something such as a plant. In a loose sense, it too has a good of its own that is much like the good of a human body. However, strictly speaking, it has no good of its own because it is not an "I." In a strict sense, a plant can at most be instrumentally good insofar as it is related to a human being (a body with a soul) that has a good of its own.

Is pleasure present in everything we enjoy?

Even if the objection to pleasure's being an unqualified good fails, there is concern of another kind about pleasure. On the view of the purpose of life that I am proposing, all pleasure is intrinsically good regardless of where or when it is experienced. But, it is asked, when one introspects, does one find something called an experience of pleasure that is common to all the activities that one finds enjoyable? Is it really plausible to hold that eating, sexual intercourse, reading a book, and watching the setting of the sun are all accompanied by instances of a type of experience that we dub "pleasure"? Or, is it more plausible to hold that all of these activities are different in their internal character and the only relevant feature that is common to them is the external relational fact that they are enjoyed by us?

Enjoyed by us for what, however? Is it really plausible to hold that the fact that we enjoy eating, sexual intercourse, reading a book, and watching the setting of the sun is itself inexplicable? Is it not more reasonable to maintain that there is an explanation of this fact and the explanation is that each activity is accompanied by the same positive feeling that we refer to as pleasure, regardless of how unlike these activities are in other respects? In short, it seems eminently reasonable to hold that pleasure is a simple and nonanalyzable qualitative experience that accompanies and makes enjoyable the otherwise diverse activities of eating, sexual intercourse, reading a book, and observing a sunset (Crisp 2006, 103–11).

Finally, some opponents of the intrinsic goodness of pleasure and the absolute use of "good" will insist that it is friendship, love, knowledge, beauty, and even the practice of philosophy itself that are intrinsically good. These things are pleasurable because they are good. They are not good because they are pleasurable.

However, one cannot help but suspect that no one would be interested in friendship, love, knowledge, beauty, etc. (they would lack attractive power), if they were not either accompanied by or productive of experiences of pleasure. The ubiquitous presence of pleasure along with all of these candidates for intrinsic goodness suggests that it, and not they, is what is intrinsically good. Consider friendship. C. S. Lewis writes that

> Friendship arises out of mere Companionship when two or more of the companions discover that they have in common some insight or interest or even taste which the others do not share and which, till that moment, each believed to be his own unique treasure (or burden). The typical expression of opening Friendship would be something like, "What? You too? I thought I was the only one (Lewis 1988, 65).

In other words, friendship is grounded in the pleasure arising out of a shared interest. Or take knowledge. Michael Ward says the following about it in his book *Planet Narnia*, where he claims to have discovered and revealed the significance of astronomy for illuminating Lewis' Narnia stories:

> Knowledge, except where it is illicit, is always a kind of pleasure, and it is hard to see how our responses to Leonardo and to the Mona Lisa would not be enriched if we could read the silent message in her lips. To prefer our former ignorance would be to adopt a Luddite or obscurantist stance. So with the Narniad: its problems of occasion, composition, and reception are, in varying degrees, "solved" by the arguments mounted in this book, and to that extent the septet no longer yields the pleasure that it used to, the pleasure we derive from thinking, "There's more going on here than meets the eye." But at the same time these explanations offer up new pleasures, first at the literary-historical level and second at the theological level. (Ward 2008, 233–4)

It is, then, the pleasure that either accompanies or is produced by instrumental goods such as friendship and knowledge that makes them attractive and the pursuit of them worthwhile, and the fact that pleasure enhances the status of these supposed intrinsic goods in this way undermines their candidacy for being intrinsic goods. Conversely, the status of pleasure as an attractive good is not enhanced by the friendship, love, knowledge, beauty, etc. that accompanies or is productive of it. Moreover, one thing that almost all proponents of the intrinsic goodness of things like friendship and love routinely fail to explain is why people are sometimes unfriendly, unloving, and more generally vicious and ignoble. What accounts for this less than ideal behavior? Surely people behave in these ways because of the allure of pleasure, and what explains the allure of pleasure is the fact that it is intrinsically good.

Conclusion

In this chapter, I have raised and answered a veritable host of objections often raised by theistic philosophers to the view that pleasure is intrinsically good and perfect happiness is the meaning of life. At the outset, I mentioned a point made by Terry Eagleton that "What is the meaning of life?" is a question in which almost every word is problematic. Not surprisingly, words used in answer to the question are equally problematic. For example, I have answered the question "What is the meaning of life?" in terms of a purpose for which we are created by God. However, many philosophers regard the idea of a purpose as deeply problematic. Indeed, they deem it so problematic that they go so far as to claim that there are no purposes for which anyone, human or divine, acts. As proponents of the doctrine of "naturalism," these philosophers conclude that everything in life can be adequately explained in terms of purposeless causes. It is to the topic of naturalism that I now turn in the next chapter.

4

Purposeful explanation and naturalism

A brief overview

This chapter includes an extended look at two topics that lie at the heart of contemporary philosophical rejections of a purpose of life. These topics are the philosophical worldview known as "naturalism" and the principle of the causal closure of the physical world that inspires it. For some readers, these matters might seem esoteric and unrelated to the purpose of life. In this case, appearances are deceptive. Institutions of higher learning are filled with naturalists who affirm the causal closure principle. As one prominent philosopher surveying the contemporary academic scene has written recently, "'Naturalism' seems to me rather like 'World Peace.' Almost everyone swears allegiance to it, and is willing to march under its banner" (Stroud 2004, 22). And another philosopher informs readers of the *New York Times* that "naturalism is popular in philosophy. In fact it is now a dominant approach in several areas of philosophy—ethics, epistemology, the philosophy of mind, philosophy of science and, most of all metaphysics, the study of the basic constituents of reality" (Rosenberg 2011). So, in a book like this one, it is imperative that I devote some significant space to naturalism and one of the most important principles that breathes life into it. Before doing this, however, I begin with an examination of the distinction between causal and purposeful explanation, because the latter is the central target of naturalism.

Looking backward versus looking forward

In his book, *What's It All About?*, Baggini says that the question "Why are we here?" invites two very different kinds of answers, when it is asked about the origins of human life. One kind of answer is future-oriented and says that human beings are caused to exist by a supernatural agent for a purpose. Baggini calls views that provide this type of answer "creationist theories" (Baggini 2004, 7). As we saw in Chapter 1, Sartre believed that the truth of this kind of answer is necessary for life to have an ultimate meaning (Sartre said that because God does not exist, life is ultimately meaningless). The other kind of answer is backward-looking and says that human beings are caused to exist for no purpose whatsoever. Baggini calls views that provide this type of answer "naturalist theories" (Baggini 2004, 7). He adds that the standard naturalist story is that the Big Bang occurred 15 billion years ago and eventually gave rise to primitive, single-celled life forms that through a process of evolution produced human beings (Baggini 2004, 7).

Like Baggini, I will simply distinguish between purposeful and causal explanations, though, strictly speaking, it is true that if God creates human beings, then they are caused to exist for a purpose. Given this strict truth, a reader might wonder why a creationist explanation is not also considered a causal explanation. The principle reason for why it is not is as follows: If a divine or human agent causes something to come to be (e.g. God creates a world or a human being makes a pie), then a natural question to ask is "What explains the causal activity of that agent?" According to a creationist theory, the causal activity of the agent (an action that causes an effect) is itself uncaused (it has no causal explanation) but is explained by a purpose (it has a teleological explanation). According to a naturalist theory, the causal activity of the agent *is* itself caused by some other event for no purpose whatsoever. A difference between the theories is that naturalists typically believe every explanation is causal in nature, while creationists believe that some explanations are causal and others are purposeful. Therefore, like Baggini, one can reasonably contrast causal explanations with purposeful explanations, with naturalists affirming the former and creationists affirming the latter, and this is the practice that I will follow in the rest of this chapter.

Baggini highlights the distinction between purposeful and causal explanations as it applies to the origin of human life at the outset of *What's It All About?* It is not until Chapter 7 of his book that he gets around to telling his reader that the same distinction is relevant to the explanation of human actions. In this later chapter, Baggini asks if we have free will, where by "free will" he means the power to make causally undetermined choices for purposes. Given that he is a materialist and atheist, he not surprisingly answers "No":

> The possibility that we don't have free will—at least as we ordinarily think of it—is not outlandish. Free will is usually thought of as the capacity to choose otherwise than we actually do [in the exact same circumstances]....
>
> But the problem is that we seem to live in a universe where every physical event has a physical cause. Furthermore, there is what is known as the "causal closure of the physical domain", meaning that everything within the physical world is caused by physical events and nothing else. Add to this the fact that all our actions involve physical movements. Even private thoughts involve physical brain events. Put these facts together and a surprising conclusion follows: all our actions must be caused entirely by events in the physical world. And because physical causation is deterministic—which means that causes necessitate their effects in some way—that leaves no room for free will. (Baggini 2004, 118–19)

Baggini goes on to point out that quantum theory in physics, which involves nondeterministic causation that makes effect events only more or less probable, is irrelevant to the issue of free will. This is because (1) quantum theory only applies to events at the subatomic level, and human beings are ordinary-size objects and (2) quantum events are random in nature, while free choices are by hypothesis nonrandom in nature.

While I have serious questions about the cogency of Baggini's first reason for dismissing the relevancy of quantum theory to the question of free will (he erroneously assumes that free will is the capacity of an ordinary-size physical object, when it is the capacity of a soul), I agree with his overall contention that it is not relevant. Therefore, in what follows I will for the most part ignore issues about quantum theory and focus my attention on the causal closure of the physical world. What I aim to show is that if purposeful explanation and the freedom of the will are real, then the physical world cannot be completely causally closed and, thus, the principle of causal closure needs to be understood differently to allow for purposeful explanations of various physical events. I will conclude that there is no problem whatsoever for a creationist theory that maintains that God creates human beings for a purpose. In other words, my contention is that in writing his book *What's It All About?* Baggini (like so many other atheists) gets things backward. Our view of the adequacy of either creationist or naturalist theories of the origins of human beings is really a function of how we view explanations of our own actions and their relationship to the principle of the causal closure of the physical world. If the causal closure principle, properly understood, does not exclude purposeful explanations of our own free choices, then there is no reason to think that it excludes the freely chosen and purposeful creation of (and intervention in) the physical world by God.

The nature of purposeful explanation

The ancient Greek philosopher, Plato, was well aware of the difference between causal and purposeful explanations. In a passage from the *Phaedo*, which is one of the numerous dialogues that Plato wrote, the principal character, Socrates, informs his interlocutor that he once heard someone reading from a book by an earlier philosopher, Anaxagoras, in which Anaxagoras claimed that it is mind (purposeful explanation) that is responsible for all things and organizes the world and its objects in the way that is best. Socrates says that he thought he had discovered, to his great pleasure, a teacher after his own persuasion. However, upon reading Anaxagoras, Socrates says he discovered a man who did not acknowledge any kind of explanatory role for the mind. Socrates' words deserve quotation in full:

And to me his [Anaxagoras'] condition seemed most similar to that of somebody who—after saying that Socrates does everything he does by mind and then venturing to assign the causes of each of the things I do—should first say that I'm now sitting here [in prison] because my body's composed of bones and sinews, and because bones are solid and have joints keeping them separate from one another, while sinews are such as to tense and relax and also wrap the bones all around along with the flesh and skin that holds them together. Then since the bones swing in their sockets, the sinews, by relaxing and tensing, make me able, I suppose, to bend my limbs right now—and it's through this cause that I'm sitting here with my legs bent. And again, as regards my conversing with you, he might assign other causes of this sort, holding voices and air and sounds and a thousand other such things responsible, and not taking care to assign the true causes—that since Athenians judged it better to condemn me, so I for my part have judged it better to sit here and more just to stay put and endure whatever penalty they order. Since—by the Dog—these sinews and bones of mine would, I think, long ago have been in Megara or Boeotia, swept off by an opinion about what's best, if I didn't think it more just and more beautiful, rather than fleeing and playing the runaway, to endure whatever penalty the city [Athens] should order. But to call such things causes is too absurd. (Plato 1998b, 98C–99A)

In most general terms, Socrates is suggesting something like the following: There are two kinds of explanation, one that is causal and another that is purposeful. When we try to explain our bodily actions, we are misguided if we think that we can ultimately explain them in terms of causes alone without any reference to purposes (ends or goals). While it is no doubt true that if Socrates had, contrary to fact, fled to Megara, then his bones and sinews would have been caused to move in certain ways, it is also true that in such a case the movements of his bones, sinews, and body to Megara would ultimately have been explained by the purpose for which Socrates was fleeing his cell in Athens. From Socrates' first-person point of view, this purpose would have been something like *that I save my life*. Moreover, as Socrates goes on to point out (Plato 1998a, 99B), there is a distinction between those things (in this case, bones, sinews, etc.) without which this purpose of saving his life could not do its explanatory work (the *necessary conditions* of the purposeful explanation) and the purpose itself. To maintain that the necessary conditions are the explanation in this case is, as Socrates claims, a most serious mistake:

> If somebody should say that I wouldn't be able to do what seemed best to me without having such things as bones and sinews and whatever else I've got, he'd be speaking the truth. If, however, he should say it was *through* these things that I'm doing what I'm doing, engaging in these acts by mind but not by the choice of what's best, why the slackness of his speech would be abundant and tedious. Imagine not being able to distinguish that it's one thing to be genuinely the cause, and another to be that without which the cause wouldn't be a cause! (Plato 1998b, 99B)

The concept of a purposeful explanation, the reality of which Socrates is affirming, is not now being introduced for the first time in this book. As I pointed out at the beginning of this chapter, I briefly discussed the concept in Chapter 1 when I presented Sartre's understanding of the question "What is the meaning of life?" and I touched upon it again in Chapter 2 when I clarified the difference between a meaning *of* life (the purpose for which a divinely created human person exists) and a meaning *in* life (the purpose for which a human person performs an action). Because purposeful explanation is so central to the position that I am defending on the meaning of life, it deserves to be explicated in a bit more detail.

As Baggini concedes (see the previous section), we ordinarily believe that we make choices to act and that we are not determined to choose as we do. Our belief is encapsulated by saying that we are not caused to choose as we do. If, by hypothesis, a choice is an undetermined event without a causal explanation, what is the explanation for its occurrence? When we are asked to give an explanation for why we choose as we do, we typically give a *reason* for our choosing that way, where a reason is a purpose. What this means is that when we choose to perform an action, we do so *in order to* accomplish or bring about a purpose. Now a choice is what philosophers call a "propositional attitude," where a propositional attitude is a mental attitude (because we have *mental* attitudes, we think of ourselves as *minds*) that is directed at or upon what is termed its "content." For example, desires, beliefs, hopes, fears, thoughts, etc. are all mental attitudes and each has content in the sense that each has as its object that something either is or come to be the case. For example, whenever one desires, one desires that such-and-such comes to be the case (e.g. I desire that I finish this section of this chapter by noon today). Whenever one believes, one believes that such-and-such is the case (e.g. I believe that it is raining outside right now). And whenever one hopes, one hopes that such-and-such come to be the case (e.g. I hope that my son and daughter will have safe trips home this coming holiday).

In general, a purposeful explanation of a choice to perform an action requires that an agent (the person making the choice) (1) represent in the content of a propositional attitude such as a belief or a desire the *future* as including a state of affairs that can be produced for the sake of its goodness; (2) represent in a belief the means to bringing about this *future* end, where the means begin with the agent performing an action; and (3) make a choice to perform that action (so the content of the choice is a description of the action to be performed) in order to bring about that *future* end.

An example is helpful at this juncture. Let us take a real-life case. Fairly recently, there has been a huge uproar in the media about the release on the internet of certain emails concerning the explanation of global warming. Some of these emails appear to indicate that certain scientists sought, among other things, to manipulate data and to exclude from peer-reviewed journals the work of other scientists who are critical of certain explanations of global warming. There is even an email that suggests that efforts might be made to call into question the professional character of one journal, if it were to publish papers critical of particular explanations of global warming. Now imagine, hypothetically, that you were aware of these emails and believed that you were morally obligated to make them the object of public knowledge. At the same time, you were in line for a large grant for your own research on global warming and believed that were you to do your moral duty and choose to release the emails, you would jeopardize the possibility of your receiving the grant. In this situation, you would have a reason to choose to release the emails, which is that you fulfill what you believe is your moral duty, and a different reason to choose not to release them, which is that you strengthen your chances of getting the grant and furthering your career. Neither reason causally determines the occurrence of the relevant choice. You will be nondeterministically free and responsible for whichever choice you make.

For purposes of clarification, I will borrow a term of art from discussions about the nature of propositional attitudes and claim that purposeful and causal explanations have what the philosopher John Searle calls different *directions of fit* (Searle 1983). The psychologist Daniel Wegner says that purposeful explanations tell us where something is headed, while causal explanations inform us about where something has been (Wegner 2002, 16). Or as Baggini suggests (Baggini 2004, 6), while a purposeful explanation is future-to-present in character (it seeks to bring that which is envisioned but not yet real into existence by present action), a causal explanation is either past-to-present in nature (what has occurred brings into existence a present event) or present-to-present in character (what is now occurring brings into existence a simultaneously occurring event). Hence, to propose, as naturalists do, a causal explanation of a choice is fundamentally to misunderstand and/or misrepresent the correct explanatory direction of that choice.

In order to do adequate justice to the issue of direction of fit, one must not only stress the idea that a reason for choosing and acting is, because of its content, a conceptual entity that is about or directed at the future but also add that it is optative (from the Latin verb *opto*, which means to wish or desire) in mood. Thus, while a reason is not a desire or a belief, the optative character of its content stems from its being grounded in the content of a desire or belief that represents a future state of affairs as good and something to be brought about by a more temporally proximate chosen action of the person who has the desire or belief.

To illustrate the optative, conceptual nature of a reason, consider the case involving the global warming emails. You believe, on the one hand, that not publishing them will strengthen your chances of getting the grant money and advancing your career and on the other hand that publishing them is morally right. For the sake of discussion, let us assume that you choose to release the emails. In light of the belief that publishing them is morally right, your reason or purpose for acting is *that you do what is morally right,* and the purposeful explanatory relation between this reason and your choice is expressed by saying that you choose to release the emails *in order to* achieve, fulfill, or bring about the purpose that you do what is morally right. If you had chosen not to release the emails because of your desire that you receive the grant money and promote your career, the content of your reason for choosing would have been *that you obtain the money and further your career*. You would have chosen *in order to* achieve or bring about the purpose that you obtain the money and advance your career.

Now let us consider two understandings of purposeful explanation that differ from mine. The first comes from the philosopher Jonathan Dancy (Dancy 2000, 114). Assume I am aware that a particular woman is ill and that I send for a doctor. Dancy maintains that it is the woman's being ill, an actual state of affairs of the world, that is my reason for sending for the doctor. Contrary to what Dancy asserts, however, it is not the woman's being ill that is my reason for sending for the doctor. Rather, my reason is the purpose that the woman be well, which is grounded in the content of a propositional attitude such as my desire that she be well (which represents a future nonactual state of affairs that can be brought into existence by means of my choosing and acting). Therefore, if I choose to send for the doctor, I do so in order to achieve or bring about the purpose that the woman be well.

The second alternative, which is really more a criticism of my kind of account of purposeful explanation than a proposed alternative understanding of this kind of explanation, comes from Baggini. I will quote him at length because doing so will facilitate my response to him:

[I]t is tempting to think that [a] "why/because" series [a series of purposeful explanations] will have to extend into the future until such time as we can stop it. However, a "why/because" series need not be temporal. For example, consider everyone's role in a restaurant. If we ask why the waiters, cooks, dishwashers, maître d', diners and so on all do what they do, the explanations will not essentially be given in terms of future goals or past events. Rather everyone is fulfilling a mutually supportive role where the activities of one meet the needs of or supply purposes for the other. Our "why" questions invite "because" answers that explain things simultaneously, as well as with regard to past or future.

Even when a "why/because" series has a temporal dimension, it need not follow one direction in time only. Consider this example:

- Why are you driving to Doncaster?
- Because I'm taking my uncle's ashes to where he wants them to be scattered (Future)
- Why are you doing that?
- Because I promised him I would (Past)
- But he's dead, so why do you feel the need to honour that promise? He'll never know.
- Because it's important to me that I'm the kind of person who keeps his word. (Present)
- Why?
- ...

In this example, aspects of the past, present and future are all used as part of the "why/because" series of justifications. This shows how it is far too limiting to see "why/because" series as having to trail off either into the past or into the future. (Baggini 2004, 26–7)

I'm confident that Baggini's examples fail to undermine the future-directed nature of the purposeful explanations of our actions. First, consider the example of you driving to Doncaster to take your uncle's ashes to the place where he wanted them scattered. Baggini says that when you are asked to explain your action, you will answer in terms of a *past* promise. But the making of this past promise is not why you are driving the ashes to Doncaster. While it is true that in the past you made a promise to drive the ashes, the explanation of your present action is directed at or concerns the future. You are acting in order to fulfill or achieve the purpose that you keep your promise. The same point applies to your explanation that it is important to you that you be the kind of person who keeps his word. Baggini says that this explanation refers to the *present*. Once again, he is mistaken. What you are saying when you appeal to being the kind of person who keeps his word is *future* in nature: you are saying that the explanation for keeping your promise is to achieve the purpose that you either continue to be or become the kind of person who keeps his word.

Similar points can be made about Baggini's example of roles in a restaurant. The explanation for why the waiters, cooks, dishwashers, etc., do what they do is future-oriented. Baggini says that everyone is fulfilling a mutually supportive role. There is no need to quarrel with this point because each person's supportive role is for the achievement of the purpose that the customer enjoy a first-rate dinner, where this achievement is something that is in the future. The cook prepares the meal, the dishwasher provides clean dinnerware, and the waiter brings the food for this purpose. Therefore, nothing that Baggini says undermines my central claim that explanations of action are essentially purposeful in nature and, thereby, directed at bringing into existence a future state of affairs that at present is not real.

Before continuing my examination of the nature of purposeful explanation, I digress briefly to consider a problem that Baggini believes arises from using the concept of a purposeful explanation of life to understand the meaning of life. According to him, the idea of a final purpose eliminates the need to do anything further, which is deeply problematic:

> So if life is to be meaningful, the "why/because" series [the series of purposeful explanations] cannot extend indefinitely into the future. At some point we have to reach an end point where a further "why" question is unnecessary, misguided or nonsensical. Otherwise the purpose of life is forever beyond our reach....
>
> But this gives rise to a further problem.... When people fulfill a lifetime's ambition they often jokingly say, "I can die happy." But this invites the serious reply, "Why not?" After all, if life is about the achievement of a goal, then once that goal is reached, what is there left to do? Once life's purpose has been fulfilled, it no longer guides our actions, apparently leaving us with nothing to live for....
>
> This illustrates how if the meaning of life is tied to goal-achievement, then achieving that goal can leave you with "emptiness"—nothing left to provide meaning.... Moments in time cannot be kept hold of, yet achievements are of their essence tied to moments of success, which all too quickly drift into the past. (Baggini 2004, 28–9)

I have proposed and defended in Chapters 1 through 3 the view that perfect happiness is the meaning of life. As the meaning of life, its achievement is the final purpose beyond which there is none other. Baggini would have us believe that the achievement of this purpose must leave us empty because there is no further purpose toward which to act. If Baggini is right, the attainment of perfect happiness, far from being the meaning of life, entails that life ends up meaningless.

The first thing to notice about Baggini's objection is the implicit assumption that the lack of anything further to *do* is problematic for life's meaning. But such an assumption is open to question. Maybe life's final purpose is not itself a doing (an action) and can be indefinitely experienced subsequent to a final doing (without the need for any further doing). In this context, it is helpful once again to invoke Robert Nozick's idea of the experience machine (Nozick 1974, 42–5), which I mentioned in previous chapters. Recall that Nozick asks his readers to imagine a machine, the programming of which will provide them with uninterrupted pleasure for as long as they wish, if they connect to it. Nozick makes clear that a person who is connected to the experience machine does not have to *do* anything. An individual never has to *act*; he or she simply experiences pleasure. Would a reasonable individual accept an offer to be connected to the experience machine?

As I pointed out in Chapter 3, readers usually wrestle with the idea of accepting the offer. On the one hand, the idea of experiencing pleasure and pleasure alone is hard for them to resist. On the other hand, the prying apart of pleasure from action leaves them puzzled because pleasure and action are so intimately connected in their own lives. They have to do something in order to experience pleasure. But as Nozick realizes, there is no nonmoral conceptual link between pleasure and action. One could have either without the other. Given that this is the case, a first answer to Baggini's objection to purposeful explanation is that achievement of a final purpose might result from an action and subsequently be sustained without the need for any further action. If the final purpose is to experience nothing except pleasure, as the example of the experience machine suggests, then achievement of this final purpose need not result in emptiness because one could indefinitely be continuously infused with experiences of nothing but pleasure, where pleasure is intrinsically good.

In a later chapter of *What's It All About?* Baggini discusses the experience machine. Like so many others, he claims not only that most people would reject the option of connecting to it, but also that they would be horrified at the idea of becoming attached to it: "The problem is that they feel they wouldn't be living a 'real' life in the machine. It is not enough to have experiences of a good life, one really wants to live a good life" (Baggini 2004, 99). Baggini goes on to assert that the example of the experience machine makes clear that we value authenticity above happiness, where authenticity involves the achievement of ends through one's own effort and, as a result, authorship of one's own life.

Unlike Baggini, I do not value authenticity above happiness. Thus, if perfect happiness were provided by an experience machine, I would connect to it. But what I would do is not at present the issue. The issue is whether achievement of a final purpose necessarily entails subsequent emptiness because of the absence of anything further to do, and the example of the experience machine makes clear that it does not.

For the sake of discussion, however, let us assume that perfect happiness as the final end is not a thorough-going passive state of affairs. Is it possible to hold that perfect happiness involves action and satisfactorily answer Baggini's objection? I believe that it is. After all, why could it not be the case that, once one has achieved the final purpose of a thoroughly pleasurable state of mind by acting, one continues to act to preserve that state of mind (where the purpose for each subsequent action is the same, vz. that one preserve one's thoroughly pleasurable state of mind)? If there is nothing incoherent in such a suggestion (and there seems not to be; cf. Chapter 2 and my discussion of Bernard Williams' argument against immortality), then it is not inevitable that emptiness follow upon the achievement of a final purpose. The fact that emptiness does sometimes follow upon achievement of a purpose in this world is no more than a contingent feature of this world. And the theist claims that it is in part this feature of this world that makes us long for a different world where this contingent feature no longer exists.

What if Baggini were now to respond that my appeal in the previous paragraph to the ongoing preservation of perfect happiness essentially amounts to a denial of the achievement of a final purpose and the affirmation of an unending series of actions in which each subsequent action is explained by the same purpose of preserving the experience of perfect happiness? In this situation, is it not the case that the purpose of life is forever beyond our reach? No. What is the case is that the purpose of life has been achieved and that actions are performed to preserve the fulfillment of that purpose.

I will have reason to return to the concept of the experience machine in Chapter 5 when I once again delve into the concept of perfect happiness. For now, I leave the matter here and pursue further issues surrounding the concept of purposeful explanation. As I pointed out earlier in this section, Baggini distinguishes between causal explanation and purposeful explanation. He also seems to concede the reality of purposeful explanation and merely questions whether it leads to problems like those we have just examined concerning (1) whether purposeful explanation is always future-oriented and (2) whether the achievement of a final purpose necessarily entails an ensuing state of emptiness. However, as I have already pointed out earlier in this section, Baggini also claims that the occurrence of *every* physical event at the level of our bodily actions has a physical cause. Now, if the occurrence of *every* bodily event has a physical cause, then it seems to follow that purposeful explanations and mental causes are not needed to explain the occurrence of those events because physical causal explanations suffice. In other words, given that the occurrence of every bodily event has a physical cause, purposeful explanations and mental causes are superfluous for explaining those events and, therefore, are either dispensable or eliminable. Hence, Baggini's talk about the reality of purposeful explanation seems to be seriously misleading.

Baggini is by no means alone in distinguishing between causal and purposeful (teleological) explanations. Kurt Baier does the same. Consider what he has to say in the following comments about the two kinds of explanation:

> When in an uninhabited forest we find what looks like houses, paved streets, temples, cooking utensils, and the like, it is no great risk to say that these things are the ruins of a deserted city, that is to say, of something manmade. In such a case, the appropriate explanation is teleological, that is, in terms of the purposes of the builders of that city. On the other hand, when a comet approaches the earth, it is similarly a safe bet that, unlike the city in the forest, it was not manufactured by intelligent creatures and that, therefore, a teleological explanation would be out of place, whereas a causal one is suitable. (Baier 2000, 104)

There are many things that a man may do, such as buying and selling, hiring labourers, ploughing, felling trees, and the like, which it is foolish, pointless, silly, perhaps crazy, to do if one has no purpose in doing them. (Baier 2000, 119)

Now, as we saw in Chapter 2, Baier distinguishes between a purpose of life (human life is the effect of a creator or God) and purposes in life (our actions are performed for purposes), and he maintains that while the former does not exist, the latter are a common feature of daily life. What explains this difference in status with respect to these two kinds of purposeful explanation? Science. With regard to purposes in life, Baier says that "acceptance of the scientific world picture does not force us to regard our lives as being without a purpose in this sense. Science has not only not robbed us of any purpose which we had before, but it has furnished us with enormously great power to achieve these purposes" (Baier 2000, 119–20). However, when it comes to a purpose of life, matters are different. According to Baier, because "science is in principle able to give complete and real explanations of every occurrence and thing in the universe" (Baier 2000, 118), there is no need for a purposeful explanation of life. What Baier means by saying that science can *in principle* provide a complete and real explanation of *every* occurrence and thing in the universe is that even if science cannot *now* provide such an explanation of something, that explanation remains only to be discovered. Moreover, an explanation is *complete* in the sense that, once it is provided, there is nothing left to be explained. And, according to Baier, a complete explanation is available for *every* occurrence and thing in the universe. But if science eliminates any need for a purposeful explanation of life, why does it not follow that it also eliminates any need for purposeful explanations in life? Given the in-principle universal scope and completeness of scientific explanation, what is there in life that is left to be explained by a purposeful explanation? The answer it seems would be "Nothing." But Baier believes that this is the wrong answer because purposeful explanations in life are themselves scientific explanations (Baier 2000, 117). But why not, then, allow for a purposeful explanation of life and deem it scientific? Because those who share Baier's conviction that there is no purpose of life think there is no good answer to this question, they believe consistency requires a denial of any purposes in life. Indeed, in their minds it is because science eliminates any need for the latter kind of purpose that it also eliminates any need for the former. Their reasoning concerning the lack of a need for purposeful explanations in life is rooted in the philosophical view known as naturalism, and it is to it that I now turn in the next section.

Naturalism

C. S. Lewis opens his book, *A Preface to Paradise Lost*, with the following admonition:

> The first qualification for judging any piece of workmanship from a corkscrew to a cathedral is to know *what* it is—what it was intended to do and how it is meant to be used. After that has been discovered the temperance reformer may decide that the corkscrew was made for a bad purpose, and the communist may think the same about the cathedral. But such questions come later. The first thing is to understand the object before you: as long as you think the corkscrew was meant for opening tins or the cathedral for entertaining tourists you can say nothing to the purpose about them. The first thing the reader needs to know about *Paradise Lost* is what Milton meant it to be. (Lewis 1942, 1)

At the outset of this chapter, I briefly mentioned Baggini's description of naturalist theories as those views of our origins that exclude purposeful explanations. However, naturalism is actually broader in scope in the sense that its subject matter includes more than views of our origins. Its explanatory reach encompasses *everything*. In other words, according to naturalism *nothing* in the physical world ultimately has an irreducible purposeful explanation. Thus, a naturalist would answer Lewis that he (Lewis) needs to understand not only that the corkscrew was not for opening tins and the cathedral not for entertaining tourists, but also that the former was not for opening wine bottles and the latter not for worshipping God. Neither was irreducibly for anything. And the purpose of *Paradise Lost*? None, according to the naturalist. Because of the extraordinary nature of these claims, it is best to let some naturalists speak for themselves.

First, consider the following thoughts that the philosophical naturalist David Papineau provides about this issue. According to Papineau, naturalism is a commitment to the completeness of physics, where physics is complete in the sense that a purely physical specification of the world, in addition to physical laws, will always suffice to explain what happens. Papineau is aware that the concepts of physics change over time. What categories, therefore, will qualify as "physical" in the final or ultimate physics? Papineau claims that we cannot answer this question with any certitude. At best, what we must do is pursue what philosophers refer to as a *via negativa*—or negative way—and specify something that will *not* qualify as physical. The "something" that Papineau suggests is the characteristic of being psychological, which is exemplified by mental attitudes such as beliefs, desires, and choices:

> When I say that a complete physics excludes psychology, and that psychological antecedents are therefore never needed to explain physical effects, the emphasis is on "needed." I am quite happy to allow that psychological categories *can* be used to explain physical effects, as when I tell you that my arm rose because I wanted to lift it. My claim is only that in all such cases an alternative specification of a sufficient antecedent [a sufficient antecedent in this context is one that guarantees the occurrence of the physical effects], which does not mention psychological categories, will also be available. (Papineau 1993, 31, footnote 26)

And again,

> If you want to use the [argument that all physical effects are fully caused by purely physical prior histories], it isn't crucial that you know exactly what a complete physics would include. Much more important is to know what it won't.
> Suppose, to illustrate the point, that we have a well-defined notion of the *mental* realm, identified via some distinctive way of picking out properties as mental. (Thus we might identify this realm as involving intentionality, say, or intelligence, or indeed as involving consciousness—the precise characterization won't matter for the point I am about to make.) Then one way of understanding "physical" would simply be as "non-mentally identifiable"—that is, as standing for properties which can be

identified independently of this specifically mental conceptual apparatus. And then, provided we can be confident that the "physical" in this sense is complete—that is, that every non-mentally identifiable effect is fully determined by *non-mentally identifiable* antecedents—then we can conclude that all mental states must be identical with (or realized by) something non-mentally identifiable (otherwise mental states couldn't have non-mentally identifiable effects). (Papineau 2002, 41)

Second, David Armstrong advocates naturalism by proposing that the ideal physics has an ultimately privileged explanatory role. According to Armstrong, naturalism is "the doctrine that reality consists of nothing but a single all-embracing spatio-temporal system" (Armstrong 1978, 261). Armstrong points out that contemporary materialism is a form of naturalism and maintains that the single all-embracing spatiotemporal system contains nothing but the entities recognized by the most mature physics. Irreducible mental explanation (explanation that involves noneliminable reference to mental causes or purposes) has no place in this (or any other) spatiotemporal system as an ultimate or basic explanatory principle. Thus, Armstrong says that "if the principles involved [in analyzing the single, all-embracing spatiotemporal system that is reality] were completely different from the current principles of physics, in particular if they involved appeal to mental entities, such as purposes, we might then count the analysis as a falsification of naturalism" (Armstrong 1978, 262).

Third, Andrew Melnyk makes it clear that naturalists in general (and he in particular) deny the reality of both irreducible mental events (mental events that cannot be analyzed in terms of parts of any kind) and irreducible teleological explanations (Melnyk 2007). As a participant in an online debate with Charles Taliaferro and me in which we claim that uncaused free choices are irreducible mental events that have fundamental teleological explanations, Melnyk denies that conscious occurrences are irreducible mental events and states that "[n]aturalism claims that nothing has a fundamental purposeful explanation.... Naturalism says that whenever an occurrence has a purposeful explanation, it has that explanation in virtue of certain nonpurposeful (e.g. merely causal) facts" (Melnyk 2007).

If we follow the lead of Papineau, Armstrong, and Melnyk, we arrive at the following position: Naturalism is the philosophical thesis that the fundamental, ultimate, or final explanatory story about the nature and course of events in the physical world will exclude any mention of what is mental in nature. *Everything* that happens in the physical world can in principle ultimately be explained without any mention of purposes. If we explain some things purposefully right now, this is only because we are at present ignorant of the fundamental physical causal explanation. With the fundamental physical causal explanation in hand, we will be able to dispense with any and every purposeful explanation. With regard to our own "actions," the naturalist Alex Rosenberg states:

> Our conscious thoughts are very crude indicators of what is going on in our brain. We fool ourselves into treating these conscious markers as thoughts about what we want and about how to achieve it, about plans and purposes. We are even tricked into thinking they somehow bring about behavior. We are mistaken about all of these things.... You cannot treat the interpretation of behavior in terms of purposes and meaning as conveying real understanding.... [T]he individual acts of human beings [are] unguided by purpose.... What individuals do, alone or together, over a moment or a month or a lifetime, is really just the product of the process of blind variation and environmental filtration operating on neural circuits in their heads. (Rosenberg 2011, 210, 213, 244, 255)

The naturalist Richard Rorty provides the following concise summary of the implications of naturalism: "Every speech, thought, theory, poem, composition and philosophy will turn out to be completely predictable in purely naturalistic terms. Some atoms-and-the-void account of micro-processes within individual human beings will permit the prediction of every sound or inscription which will ever be uttered" (Rorty 1979, 387). The implication of naturalism is that not one word of Rosenberg's and Rorty's books is written for a purpose, not even the purpose of defending naturalism.

What justifies the adoption of such an extraordinary position? Why believe it is true? The answer to these questions can be found in Baggini's discussion of the idea of causal closure. According to Baggini, "we seem to live in a universe where every physical event has a physical cause. Furthermore, there is what is known as the 'causal closure of the physical domain', meaning that everything within the physical world is caused by physical events and nothing else" (Baggini 2004, 118). Given the apparent implications of causal closure for purposeful explanation (e.g. not only is there no purpose of life, but also there are no purposes in life), why should/ would anyone believe in the causal closure of the physical world? In the next section, I explain what the naturalist has to say in answer to this question and why this answer is mistaken.

The causal closure principle

As I pointed out at the beginning of this chapter, Baggini recognizes that our ordinary conception of ourselves includes the belief that we have nondeterministic free will (we make undetermined free choices). Baggini also recognizes that our ordinary conception of ourselves includes the belief that we are or have souls and that it is they that make the nondeterministic choices that are free (Baggini 2004, Chapter 9). To understand how these ordinary beliefs are related to the principle of the causal closure of the physical world, consider the movements of my fingers right now on the keys of my keyboard as I work on this chapter. If these movements occur because of a choice of mine to type, then these physical movements are ultimately and irreducibly explained in terms of the purpose for which I chose to write this chapter, which is that I make clear that the causal closure argument is not a solid objection to the view that there is a purpose of life and that we act for purposes. Hence, if the movements of my fingers are ultimately occurring because I made a choice to write this chapter for a purpose, then a mental event involving me (a soul) must be *causing* those movements to occur. In short, if the commonsense view of a human being is correct, I, as a soul, am causing events to occur in the physical world by making a choice to write this chapter for a purpose.

From the example of my typing, it should be clear that the claim that there is causal interaction between a soul and its physical body is *not* a "God-of-the-gaps" type of argument. In discussions about God's existence, critics often argue that theists *postulate* God's existence in light of an inability of science to provide a complete explanation for a physical datum (or data). For example, Michael Behe, one of the foremost spokespersons for what has become known as intelligent design, argues that, in light of what he refers to as the irreducible complexity of the bacterial flagellum, it cannot reasonably be held that nonpurposeful evolutionary forces alone working through time produced the existence of this biological organ. On the contrary, the existence of an intelligent designer acting for a purpose must be postulated to explain its existence (Behe 1996). And this lack of a complete explanation in physical causal terms implies a gap in the scientific story.

It is not my purpose to assess the cogency of Behe's argument (indeed, given my lack of knowledge of molecular biology, I cannot assess it). Rather, it is to point out that an advocate of causal closure might suggest that I am postulating my soul's existence in light of an inability of science so far to provide a complete physical causal explanation for the movements of my fingers when I type this essay. In other words, just as there are God-of-the-gaps arguments, so also there are soul-of-the-gaps arguments. But this suggestion would be mistaken. My claim is *not* that there are certain physical events (the movements of my fingers) for which a failure to find a complete physical causal story warrants appeal to the causal activity of a soul for their ultimate explanation. Rather, my claim is that our purposeful activity entails that some physical events must occur whose ultimate causal explanation is not other physical events but nonphysical mental events whose occurrences are themselves explained by purposes.

What, then, is wrong with this commonsense understanding of a human being? According to many philosophers, a serious problem for the view that souls make choices that causally produce events in physical bodies arises out of the practice of science. Richard Taylor puts forth a lengthy argument, the gist of which is as follows:

> Consider some clear and simple case of what would ... constitute the action of the mind upon the body. Suppose, for example, that I am dwelling in my thought upon high and precarious places, all the while knowing that I am really safely ensconced in my armchair. I imagine, perhaps, that I am picking my way along a precipice and visualize the destruction that awaits me far below in case I make the smallest slip. Soon, simply as the result of these thoughts and images, ... perspiration appears on the palms of my hands. Now here is surely a case, if there is any, of something purely mental ... and outside the realm of physical nature bringing about observable physical changes. ... Here, ... one wants to say, the mind acts upon the body, producing perspiration.

But what actually happens, alas, is not nearly so simple as this. To say that thoughts in the mind produce sweat on the hands is to simplify the situation so grossly as hardly to approximate any truth at all of what actually happens.... The perspiration ... is secreted by tiny, complex glands in the skin. They are caused to secrete this substance, not by any mind acting on them, but by the contraction of little unstriated muscles. These tiny muscles are composed of numerous minute cells, wherein occur chemical reactions of the most baffling complexity.... These ... connect eventually, and in the most dreadfully complicated way, with the hypothalamus, a delicate part of the brain that is centrally involved in the emotional reactions of the organism .... [B]ut it is not seriously considered by those who do know something about it that mental events must be included in the description of its operations. The hypothalamus, in turn, is closely connected with the cortex and subcortical areas of the brain, so that physical and chemical changes within these areas produce corresponding physical effects within the hypothalamus, which in turn, by a series of physical processes whose complexity has only barely been suggested, produces such remote effects as the secretion of perspiration on the surface of the hands.

Such, in the barest outline, is something of the chemistry and physics of emotional perspiration.... The important point, however, is that in describing it as best we can, there is no need, at any stage, to introduce mental or nonphysical substances or reactions. (Taylor 1992, 20–2)

According to Taylor, while we are inclined to believe that certain physical events in our bodies are ultimately explained by mental events of nonphysical substances, as a matter of fact there is no need at any point to step outside of the physical causal story to explain the occurrences of those physical events. Another philosopher, Jaegwon Kim, uses an example of a neuroscientist to make the same point:

You want [or choose] to raise your arm, and your arm goes up. Presumably, nerve impulses reaching appropriate muscles in your arm made those muscles contract, and that's how the arm went up. And these nerve signals presumably originated in the activation of certain neurons in your brain. What caused those neurons to fire? We now have a quite detailed understanding of the process that leads to the firing of a neuron, in terms of complex electrochemical processes involving ions in the fluid inside and outside a neuron, differences in voltage across cell membranes, and so forth. All in all we seem to have a pretty good picture of the processes at this microlevel on the basis of the known laws of physics, chemistry, and biology. If the immaterial mind is going to cause a neuron to emit a signal (or prevent it from doing so), it must somehow intervene in these electrochemical processes. But how could that happen? At the very interface between the mental and the physical where direct and unmediated mind-body interaction takes place, the nonphysical mind must somehow influence the state of some molecules, perhaps by electrically charging them or nudging them this way or that way. Is this really conceivable? Surely the working neuroscientist does not believe that to have a complete understanding of these complex processes she needs to include in her account the workings of immaterial souls and how they influence the molecular processes involved.... Even if the idea of a soul's influencing the motion of a molecule ... were coherent, the postulation of such a causal agent would seem neither necessary nor helpful in understanding why and how our limbs move.... Most physicalists ... accept the causal closure of the physical not only as a fundamental metaphysical doctrine but as an indispensable methodological presupposition of the physical sciences.... If the causal closure of the physical domain is to be respected, it seems prima facie that mental causation must be ruled out .... (Kim 1996, 131–2, 147–8)

While Kim agrees with Taylor about the lack of a need on the part of a scientist to go outside the physical explanatory story, he introduces the stronger idea that to be successful the physical sciences need to make the methodological assumption of the causal closure of the physical world. Is he right about this?

To ensure clarity about what is at issue, consider one more example of movements of my body that according to common sense could only be adequately explained by mental causation of a soul whose choice is explained by a purpose or reason. Just this morning, I was asked to give the eulogy at a memorial service for the former president of the college where I teach. He was a very close friend and I am mulling over what I will say in my talk for the purpose of honoring him. If the physical world is causally closed, I will neither write nor deliver the eulogy for a purpose, nor will those who attend the service be there for a purpose. As I speak, the movements of my mouth will be completely explicable in terms of physical goings-on that occur in my brain and body, none of which need be explained in terms of the purpose for which it seems I am acting. Now, this seems simply crazy because reference to my mental activity and my purposes for writing and giving the eulogy appear to be not only helpful but also necessary to explain both the movements of my fingers on the keyboard while I am typing and the movements of my mouth as I deliver my address. If we assume that I, as a soul, cause my fingers and mouth to move by directly causing some neural events in the motor section of my brain, then when I move my fingers and move my mouth for purposes, I must directly cause initial neural events in my brain that ultimately lead to the movements of these bodily parts. In other words, in order to explain adequately (purposefully) the movements of these bodily parts, there must be causal openness in the form of a causal gap in my brain.

While Kim believes that the commonsense view of my actions implies this causal openness in the physical world, he also believes that it is because the commonsense view implies the existence of this causal gap that it must be mistaken. Because the neuroscientist methodologically assumes causal closure of the physical world, what he discovers as the explanation for what occurs in my brain and limbs when I type and give the eulogy must not include reference to the mental causal activity of my soul and the ultimate and irreducible explanatory purpose for which I choose to act. Given that the principle of causal closure as understood by Kim entails the exclusion of a soul's mental causation of a physical event and the ultimate and irreducible teleological explanation of that mental event and its effects by a purpose, it is imperative that we examine the argument from causal closure to see if it provides a good reason to believe that the movements of my fingers and mouth when I am typing and speaking must be *completely* explicable in terms of neuroscience (or any other physical science), with the result that no reference to the causal activity of my soul and its purposes for moving my fingers and mouth is, in the end, required.

Before conducting this examination, it is only fair to point out that Kim also recognizes the counterintuitive nature of the conclusion of the argument from causal closure, which is that our mental lives have no explanatory role to play in accounting for events in the physical world (our mental lives are what philosophers call explanatorily *epiphenomenal*). Hence, in order to preserve an explanatory role for the mental, he believes that we should be committed to a reduction of the mental to the physical in which anything that is mental is ultimately just made up of that which is physical and, as a result, has a complete physical explanation:

> Mind-to-body causation is fundamental if our mentality is to make a difference to what goes on in the world. If I want to have the slightest causal influence on anything outside me—to change a light bulb or start a war—I must first move my limbs or other parts of my body; somehow, my beliefs and desires must cause the muscles in my arms and legs to contract, or cause my vocal cords to vibrate. Mental causation is fundamental to our conception of mentality, and to our view of ourselves as agents ... ; any theory of mind that is not able to accommodate mental causation must be considered inadequate, or at best incomplete.... Does this mean that we are committed willy-nilly to reductionism? The answer is no: what we have established ... is a *conditional* thesis, "If mentality is to have any causal efficacy at all—it must be physically reducible." Those of us who believe in mental causation should hope for a successful reduction. (Kim 2005, 152–3, 161)

According to Kim, then, physical reduction enables us to preserve our belief that what goes on in our mental lives makes a causal explanatory difference to the course of events in the physical world. We should notice, however, the price that must be paid to embrace this "solution" to the problem of causal closure. Mentality can make an explanatory difference only if we give up both the idea that mental actions are ultimately and irreducibly explained by purposes and the view that we make choices that are not causally determined. We must give up on both of these ideas because the physical events to which a mental event is reduced are themselves causally determined by other physical events that occur for no purpose whatsoever. While Kim is correct when he insists that none of us wants to give up on the idea of mental causation, some of us also find it difficult to give up the idea that mental causation itself occurs because mental actions such as choices are nondeterministic events that are ultimately and irreducibly explained by purposes.

Given the high price that must be paid to endorse Kim's "solution" to the problem that is supposedly created by the causal closure principle, it is advisable to examine both the principle and the problem it supposedly creates. Contrary to what Kim maintains, there is good reason to think that there is no genuine problem. To explain why this is the case, I will distinguish between a neuroscientist as an *ordinary human being* and a neuroscientist as a *physical scientist*. Surely a neuroscientist, as an ordinary human being who is trying to understand the how and why of my bodily movements when I am writing and then delivering the eulogy, would refer to me and my reasons (purposes) for acting in a complete account of why my limbs move (here, one should recall the mention earlier in this chapter of Socrates' discussion of what is an adequate explanation of his not fleeing from jail). Likewise, when, as an everyday person, the neuroscientist is considering his own work as a neuroscientist, he will view that work as purposeful in nature. Kim tells us that he must avoid invoking a teleological explanation in his work because as a physical scientist he must make a methodological assumption about the causal closure of the physical world. Is Kim right about this and, if he is, is such a commitment compatible with a commitment on the part of a physical scientist as an ordinary human being to causal openness? Or must a neuroscientist, who as a physical scientist assumes causal closure, also assume, if he is consistent, that as an ordinary human being, his mention of choices and their teleological explanations is no more than a heuristic explanatory device that is necessary as long as there is a gap in his knowledge of the physical causes of human behavior?

In order to answer these questions, it is necessary to consider what it is about physical entities that a physical scientist such as a neuroscientist is often trying to discover in his experimental work. What is the purpose of a neuroscientist's inquiry? In the case of Kim's neuroscientist, what he is trying to discover as a physical scientist are the capacities of particles or micro-physical entities such as neurons to be causally affected by exercised causal powers of other physical entities, including other neurons. For example, in his pioneering work on the brain, Wilder Penfield produced movements in the limbs of his patients by stimulating their cortical motor areas with an electrode (Penfield 1975). As Penfield observed the neural impulses that resulted from stimulation by the electrode, he had to assume *during his experiments* that the areas of the brains of his patients on whom he was doing his scientific work were causally closed to other causal influences. Without this methodological assumption, he could not conclude both that it was the electrode (as opposed, say, to something "behind the scene" such as an empirically undetectable human soul, either that of the patient or someone else, or God) that causally affected the capacities of the neurons to conduct electrical impulses and that it was the impulses of those neurons that causally affected the same capacities of other neurons farther down the causal chains to produce the movements of the limbs. There is no reason, however, to think that because Penfield's investigation of the brain required the methodological assumption of causal closure of the areas of the brains he was studying during his experiments that he also had to be committed as a physical scientist to the assumption that the physical world is *universally* causally closed, where universal causal closure entails that the relevant brain (neural) events can *only* be causally produced by events of other physical entities, and not instead by mental events of immaterial souls alone when they nondeterministically choose and intend to act for purposes. That is, there is no reason to think that because a neuroscientist like Penfield must assume causal closure of a delimited area of the brain in the context of his experimental work in order to discover how physical entities causally interact with each other that he must also be committed as a scientist to the universal explanatory exclusion of mental events of souls that on certain occasions cause the occurrences of events in the physical world. All that the neuroscientist as a physical scientist must assume is that, during his experiments, souls (either of the patients themselves or of others) are not causally producing the relevant events in the microphysical entities in the areas of the brain that he is studying. If the neuroscientist makes the universal assumption that in *any* context events in microphysical entities can only have other physical events as causes and can never be causally explained by mental events of souls with their purposes, then he does so not as a scientist but as a naturalist who believes that the occurrence of physical events can only be explained in terms of the occurrence of other physical events and without any reference to ultimate and irreducible purposes of souls.

It is important to point out in this context that Penfield himself was not a naturalist. Rather, he was a soul-body dualist (Penfield 1975, 76, 80). One must surmise, then, that were Penfield to have been presented with the argument from causal closure, he would have found it unconvincing. And for good reason. In seeking to understand how events of different physical entities affect the capacities of micro-entities, such as neurons, a neuroscientist, such as Penfield, is seeking to learn about properties of physical entities that are essentially *conditional* or *iffy* in nature. A conditional property of an object is one that is specified in terms such as "If such-and-such is done to object O (e.g. a cause C is exerted on O), then so-and-so will occur to O (e.g. O will move at rate R)." As the Nobel physicist Richard Feynman says, scientific questions are "questions that you can put this way: 'if I do this, what will happen?' ... And so the question 'If I do it what will happen?' is a typically scientific question" (Feynman 1998, 16, 45). The following description by the philosopher David Chalmers of basic particles that are studied by physicists nicely captures their iffy nature:

> Basic particles ... are largely characterized in terms of their propensity to interact with other particles. Their mass and charge is specified, to be sure, but all that a specification of mass ultimately comes to is a propensity to be accelerated in certain ways [moved at certain rates] by forces, and so on. ... Reference to the proton is fixed as the thing that causes interactions of a certain kind that combines in certain ways with other entities, and so on .... (Chalmers 1996, 153)

What Chalmers describes as a "propensity" of a particle to be accelerated is a capacity of it to be moved that is such that *if* it is actualized (triggered) by an exercised causal power of another entity (whether physical or nonphysical in nature), the particle will be necessitated to behave in a certain way. There is nothing, however, in the nature of the propensity or capacity of that particle that entails that it can only be actualized by the exercised power of a physical entity. That is, there is nothing in the nature of that propensity or capacity that entails that it cannot be actualized by persons making undetermined choices for reasons. Hence, the actualization of a microparticle's capacity to behave in a certain way by a person on an occasion when the latter makes a choice for a reason is not excluded by anything that is discovered in a scientific study of that capacity. And it is precisely on occasions like those noted by Kim, when finger and lip movements seemingly occur for purposes, that a neuroscientist will reasonably believe that the originative microphysical movements are traceable to the causal activity of a soul that is choosing to act for a purpose. If a neuroscientist makes the presupposition that microphysical entities can have their capacities actualized *only* by other physical entities and never by choices made by souls for purposes, then he does so as a naturalist and not as a scientist.

My response to the causal closure argument assumes Feynman's and Chalmers' iffy picture of micro-entities that, in addition to being iffy, is also deterministic in the sense that no effect will occur in any micro-entity unless some causal event determines or necessitates that effect to take place. Might there not, however, be random (indeterministic) changes in the system of micro-entities as well as the deterministic ones? In other words, while sometimes a neuron fires because it gets deterministic causal input from the neurons with which it is connected, at other times it fires at random (without any deterministic cause), perhaps as a result of random quantum fluctuations in a chaotic system that are magnified at the neuronal level.

If we assume for the sake of discussion that neurons do sometimes fire randomly, is it possible to distinguish clearly between those firings that occur randomly and those that occur as the result of being causally determined by a mental event of a soul? After all, the two kinds of firing are alike to the extent that neither has a physically deterministic cause. Given that they are indistinguishable in this way, can they be reasonably distinguished in some other way that will enable us to conclude that certain firings are ultimately purposeful in nature? I believe that it is possible to make this sharp distinction between the two kinds of firings. The way to make the distinction is in terms of contexts that are known, in the case of ourselves, through first-person experience and, in the case of others, through third-person observation. All one needs to do is ask how plausible it is to maintain that every time a person purposefully chooses to do something such as either move his fingers to type or move his mouth to talk, an initial firing of a neuron just happens to occur at random (as a result of quantum fluctuations, etc.) with the result that finger or mouth movements occur that perfectly mesh with those that are intended by that person for a purpose. Because such repeated coincidences would literally be, shall we say, miraculous, the only plausible view is that the neuron must not be firing randomly but because of the causal input from a soul choosing and intending to act for a purpose.

Because the argument of the preceding pages has been somewhat technical, it is important to step back and clarify at a more general level how the issue of the causal closure of the physical world is related to the question of life's meaning. Most generally, what must be made clear is that if the reality of our choosing and acting for purposes is undermined by the causal closure argument, then the idea that each of us is created by God for a purpose is equally problematic. After all, the argument from causal closure is species neutral in the sense that, if it is sound, it excludes purposeful explanations of physical events, period, regardless of whether or not the purposes are those of human or divine beings. Thus, it is not in the least surprising to find atheists employing the causal closure argument in an effort to discredit the idea that God caused the physical world to exist and can cause events to occur in it for purposes. As examples of atheists who make use of the argument from causal closure, consider the following comments of J. B. S. Haldane, Douglas Futuyma, and Matthew Bagger:

My practice as a scientist is atheistic. That is to say, when I set up an experiment I assume that no god, angel or devil is going to interfere with its course .... I should therefore be intellectually dishonest if I were not also atheistic in the affairs of the world. (Haldane in Krauss 2009)

Science is the exercise of reason, and so is limited to questions that can be approached by the use of reason, questions that can be answered by the discovery of objective knowledge and the elucidation of natural laws of causation. In dealing with questions about the natural world, scientists must act as if they can be answered without recourse to supernatural powers ... of God. (Futuyma 1982, 169–70)

[W]e can never assert that, in principle, an event resists naturalistic [physical] explanation. A perfectly substantial, anomalous event, rather than providing evidence for the supernatural, merely calls into question our understanding of particular laws. In the modern era, this position fairly accurately represents the educated response to novelty. Rather than invoke the supernatural, we can always adjust our knowledge of the natural in extreme cases.

In the modern age in actual inquiry, we never reach the point where we throw up our hands and appeal to divine intervention to explain a localized event like an extraordinary experience. (Bagger 1999, 13)

Recently, Pope Benedict XVI stated that "[the] universe is not the result of chance, as some would want to make us believe" (Pope Benedict XVI 2011). What Benedict believes is that God caused the universe to exist for a purpose. As I will briefly suggest in the penultimate section of this chapter and argue in more depth in the next, God caused the universe to exist, at least in part, for the purpose of providing a setting in which human beings are able to make undetermined choices that will determine whether or not they will receive the perfect happiness for which they were created. Now, if whether or not there is a purpose of life hinges on whether or not God creates human beings and their world, then that world had better not be causally closed to divine causation. And if whether or not individuals fulfill the purpose of life for which they were created is a function of the purposeful choices that they make in this life, where those choices causally affect the course of events in the physical world, then the physical world must not be closed to causation by human souls. And the practice of science provides no reason to believe that it is closed.

In summary, then, if the argument from causal closure cannot be answered when it is directed at excluding human souls and their purposes in life, then it cannot be answered when it is directed at excluding God's activity in the form of a purpose of life. But, if I am right, the argument can be answered in the latter case in the same way that it can be answered in the former, which is in terms of the distinction between a scientist as a physical scientist and a scientist as an ordinary human being. Thus, using Haldane as our example, he is mistaken when he claims that his atheism, in the form of his employing the causal closure principle in his experimental work, must, lest he be intellectually dishonest, carry over into his daily life outside the laboratory. What is true is that he would be intellectually dishonest in failing to carry his atheism from the laboratory into his daily life, if he were a naturalist. But his practice as a physical scientist does not require that he be a naturalist. His science requires "atheism" in the form of his employment of the causal closure principle only within the context of his scientific work. Once he steps outside that context into everyday life, there is no need for him to take his "atheism" along with him. In short, nothing about the scientist's need for the assumption of causal closure within his or her work as a physical scientist entails that there is no room for purposeful explanations in or of life. Just as there is room for purposeful human activity, so also there is room for purposeful divine activity.

Science is not the problem

In the previous section, I contrasted what a scientist thinks about causal closure as a scientist with what he or she thinks about it as a naturalist. I argued that the need to universally reject the causal openness of the physical world to purposeful explanations does not come from science but from naturalism and that being a scientist does not require being a naturalist. However, it is common for opponents of the view that God has created human beings with a purpose of life to argue that science is *the* problem for the meaningfulness of life. For example, in "Man against Darkness," Walter T. Stace argues that science has informed us that "the world which surrounds us is nothing but an immense spiritual emptiness. It is a dead universe. We do not live in a universe which is on the side of our values. It is completely indifferent to them" (Stace 2000, 84).

But what is it about science that has yielded this picture of the universe? According to Stace, it is tempting to think that one or more particular scientific theories or discoveries (e.g. the Darwinian theory of evolution or geological discoveries that suggest the earth is extremely old) have proven to be the death-knell for the belief in a universe that is for, and not against, us and our values. But, says Stace, to believe this would be a mistake. The view that God has created us for a purpose is probably compatible with any particular scientific theory or discovery. What is problematic is the assumption by scientists of all stripes

> that inquiry into purposes is useless for what science aims at: namely, the prediction and control of events.... Hence science from the seventeenth century onwards became exclusively an inquiry into causes. The conception of purpose in the world was ignored and frowned on. This, though silent and almost unnoticed, was the greatest revolution in human history .... It

is this which has killed religion.... Religion can get on with any sort of astronomy, geology, biology, physics. But it cannot get on with a purposeless and meaningless universe. If the scheme of things is purposeless and meaningless, then the life of man is purposeless and meaningless.... A man may, of course, still pursue disconnected ends, money, fame, art, science, and may gain pleasure from them. But his life is hollow at the center. (Stace 2000, 86–7)

Stace's mention of pleasure is interesting, given my thesis about the purpose of life. But that is not my concern here. I am presently interested in the relationship between naturalism, science, and purposeful explanation. In light of my argument in the previous section, Stace is right to claim that the religious picture of human life can withstand particular developments in astronomy, geology, biology, and physics that invoke causal explanations that do not conflict with the idea that we are made for a purpose and act purposefully. But if this is the case, why think science's exclusive use of causal explanation yields a belief in a purposeless and meaningless universe? Stace says that even while living in a purposeless and meaningless universe, a man may "of course" still pursue purposes such as money, fame, art, and science itself. But if science describes a physical world that is causally open to purposeful explanations in life, there is no reason to think that this world is not also causally open to a purposeful explanation of life. This is the conclusion of my argument in the previous section. In other words, contrary to what Stace says, science presents no problem for a religious understanding of life (that there is a purpose of life). Science and religion are thoroughly compatible. What is the problem for a religious view of life is naturalism, and the reader must always be aware that those who, like Stace, claim that science eliminates a purpose of life are likely either knowingly or unknowingly substituting naturalism for science. While naturalism kills religion, science does not, because while the former insists that everything is causally explicable in purposeless, physical terms, the latter does not. Though science does provide causal explanations of what it explains, it does not insist that everything be causally explained. Only naturalism does that. And while religion cannot survive without purposeful explanation, science can survive without naturalism because science can survive without the assumption of universal causal closure, as I argued in the previous section.

Survival or pleasure:
what explains what?

As I mentioned early on in this chapter, naturalists like Baggini typically deny that we have free will in the sense that we make undetermined choices. As a naturalist, Baggini believes that any kind of free will that we have must be *compatible* with the truth of causal determinism. (Philosophers like Baggini are known as *compatibilists*, and they typically maintain that a bodily movement [e.g. an arm movement], though determined, is free when it is caused by beliefs and desires, which are themselves causally determined.) Moreover, most naturalists today are also evolutionary naturalists who believe that the survival of some organisms and the demise of others are explained nonpurposefully by natural selection working on random genetic mutations. A question that some evolutionary naturalists seek to answer is "Why do we have free will?" According to the evolutionary naturalist Roy F. Baumeister, a person's possession of free will is explained in terms of its being advantageous for survival. In Baumeister's words, free will helped humans

> to create and sustain culture and to survive and reproduce effectively in a cultural environment....
>
> What is culture? ... In general, ... culture is understood as an information-based system that enables people to live together in organized fashion and to satisfy their basic needs, ultimately including survival and reproduction.
>
> Culture is ... humankinds's biological strategy. It is how our species solves the universal problems of survival and reproduction. (Baumeister 2010, 25)

I raise the question "Why do we have free will?" because an evolutionary naturalist's answer to this question (we have free will because it promotes survival) likely indicates the way in which he or she views the relationship between pleasure (happiness) and survival. For example, the evolutionary naturalist Daniel Dennett asks why it is that humans expend so much effort to acquire things such as food and drink that are sweet, and he answers that our distant ancestors discovered that a food substance such as sugar is a great source of energy, so that they, with their preference for and ability to ingest sugar, were better able to survive than other beings that did not possess this preference and ability. Dennett says it is natural to think that our distant ancestors liked sugar for its sweetness (i.e. for the pleasure that it gives). However, as an evolutionary naturalist, he insists that what is natural to believe in this case is mistaken and gets things backward: "People generally say that we like some things because they are sweet, but this really puts it backward: it is more accurate to say that some things are sweet (to us) because we like them! (And *we* like them because our ancestors who were wired up to like them had more energy for reproduction than their less fortunately wired-up peers)" (Dennett 2006, 59; cf. Wilson 2002, 170–2).

Where, then, does pleasure fit into all of this? And what of its intrinsic goodness? According to Dennett, "'intrinsic' value is the capacity of something to provoke a preference response in the brain quite directly. Pain is 'intrinsically bad,' but this negative valence is … dependent on an evolutionary rationale" (Dennett 2006, 68–9). When it comes to questions about value, "[b]iology insists on delving beneath the surface of 'intrinsic' values and asking why they exist, and any answer that is supported by the facts has the effect of showing that the value in question is—or once was—really instrumental, not intrinsic, even if we don't see it that way" (Dennett 2006, 69). As Dennett goes on to note (Dennett 2006, 69), if something really had intrinsic value (e.g. if it really were intrinsically good), then there would be no explanation for its being so. It would necessarily just have the value that it has. Because, however, the naturalistic evolutionary explanatory story is fundamental, any value must be explicable in terms of causation that is productive of survival, regardless of how things seem to us. So according to Dennett, pleasure cannot be intrinsically good, even though it seems to us to be so. The value of it is no more than instrumental in nature. Dennett would also insist that happiness is not intrinsically good (assuming that it is made up of experiences of pleasure) and would most certainly claim that perfect happiness cannot be the purpose for which we exist.

Evolutionary naturalists like Dennett maintain that nothing is intrinsically good. Because of this belief, it seems only right that they would also claim that nothing is instrumentally good. After all, something is instrumentally good only if it ultimately leads to the production of what is intrinsically good (or the prevention, diminishment, or elimination of what is intrinsically evil). So if someone like Dennett were to talk about something's being "instrumentally good," what would he mean by saying this? Most likely, what he would mean is that this something promotes survival. "Good" would mean "has survival value." Thus, when the evolutionary naturalist Richard Dawkins writes about the sweetness of sugar, he says that "sweet taste in the mouth ... [is] going to be 'good' in the sense that eating sugar ... [is] likely to be beneficial to gene survival" (Dawkins 1989, 57). Survival, however, just is or occurs and has no value (see below). Most certainly, it is not good in and of itself. In a chapter entitled "Why are people?" Dawkins maintains that

> Darwin made it possible for us to give a sensible answer ["survival"] to the curious child whose question ["Why are people?"] heads this chapter. We no longer have to resort to superstition when faced with deep problems: Is there meaning to life? What are we for? ... Philosophy and the subjects known as "humanities" are still taught almost as if Darwin had never lived. (Dawkins 1989, 1)

In light of Darwin, we no longer have to resort to superstition when faced with deep problems like the meaning of life. What counts as superstition? As we have seen earlier in this chapter, naturalists believe it is possible in principle to give a complete explanation of anything and everything in causal terms that make no reference to the idea of purpose. Hence, it is not much of a stretch to conclude that evolutionary naturalists regard any mention of purpose as superstition. As Thomas Nagel points out,

> [E]volutionary naturalism is radically antiteleological. This implies that it is not suited to supply any kind of sense to our existence, if it is taken on as the larger perspective from which life is lived. Instead, the evolutionary perspective probably makes human life, like all life, meaningless, since it makes life a more or less accidental consequence of physics. (Nagel 2010, 15)

Evolutionary naturalism is not suited to provide any sense to our existence that is purposeful in nature. Because the evolutionary naturalist accepts the universal causal closure of the physical

world and the exclusion of teleological explanations, he or she is
driven to deny the intrinsic goodness of pleasure that ultimately
provides the basis for purposeful explanations. However, if, as I
have argued, there is no good reason to accept the universal causal
closure of the physical world, then the evolutionary naturalist will
have to provide some other reason to convince us that pleasure
is not intrinsically good and does not occupy the place it seems
to occupy in purposeful explanations. What is interesting to note
at this juncture is that Darwin himself found it hard to shake our
ordinary convictions about pleasure. After noting that the country
of Tierra del Fuego at the tip of South America "is a broken mass
of wild rock, lofty hills, and useless forests" and adding that the
"habitable land is reduced to the stones which form the beach,"
Darwin wondered "[w]hat could have tempted, or what change
compelled a tribe of men ... to enter on one of the most inhospitable
countries within the limits of the globe?" and answered that "[W]e
must suppose that they enjoy a sufficient share of happiness (of
whatever kind it may be) to render life worth living" (Darwin 1989,
178–9). So according to Darwin's hypothesis taken at face value,
the Fuegons believed it was worthwhile surviving for the purpose of
experiencing happiness. Happiness explained survival in the case of
the Fuegons, instead of the other way around. Darwin's supposition
about the Fuegons undoubtedly stemmed from his own experiences
of what is intrinsically good. For example, his description of his own
feelings upon beholding the beauty of a Brazilian forest included the
following: "To a person fond of natural history, such a day as this
brings with it a deeper pleasure than he can ever hope to experience
again" (Darwin 1989, 50).

The antiteleological character of evolutionary naturalism leads
proponents of it like Dennett and Dawkins to deny what seems
to be the case about pleasure and its intrinsic goodness. There is
another consideration that undermines such a denial, which is the
fact that the occurrence of pleasure in an evolutionary naturalistic
world is difficult to explain.

To clarify what I have in mind, consider a standard example
of how natural selection works on random (nonpurposeful)
genetic changes. This example involves finches (Futuyma 1982,
119). In 1977, a drought occurred in the Galapagos Islands that
resulted in a shortage of small seeds on which the finches there
fed. To survive, the finches had to eat bigger seeds that they up

till then had normally overlooked. After a generation, most of the smaller finches died because they could not eat the larger seeds. Thus, the average size of the birds, and especially the size of their beaks (a phenotypical feature), went up because only the larger birds remained to reproduce and pass on the originally randomly produced genetic message (a genotypical feature) for this larger size beak. In this instance, being the fittest to survive meant having the genes that produced the bigger beak.

In this example, the conceptual categories are spatial and part-whole in nature. That is, a spatial alteration in genes at the micro level resulted in bigger wholes (arranged parts that constitute beaks) at the macro level. These changes enhanced the opportunity for survival of the finches with the bigger beaks. Now consider experiences of pleasure. How could they come to be? The problem for the evolutionary naturalist is that experiences of pleasure are not things like beaks that are wholes made up of parts. Experiences of pleasure are events that seem to be simple in nature (they have no event parts). How might random genetic change give rise to organisms with the capacity to experience such events? Unless we are to believe that the ultimate material constituents of the physical world possessed such a capacity from the outset (a position known in philosophy as panpsychism—psychological properties like the capacity to experience pleasure are possessed by the ultimate constituents of the physical world), evolutionary naturalists seem forced to conclude that nonpsychic physical entities *somehow* managed, when combined, to constitute a physical entity with a new kind of property, the capacity to experience pleasure.

At this point in time, evolutionary naturalists do not have any explanation, and certainly not one that employs spatial part-whole categories, for how the capacity to experience pleasure came to be from a combination of objects that were thoroughly nonpsychic in nature. Some evolutionary naturalists talk or write as if they have a just-so story about the origin of this capacity, where a just-so story is an account that says something like "things might have developed in such-and-such a way." For example, Owen Flanagan says the following:

> Among philosophers and scientists who accept the neo-Darwinian theory and thus accept that sentience evolved from insensate life (bacteria for whom "there was nothing it is/was like to be them"),

there are only stories, some more credible than others, as to why evolution favored an engineering solution that, across many distinct lineages, produced sentience. No really good view of how and why (these being different questions) it happened has been satisfactorily worked out.... But as regards the evolution of sentience, we are pretty much, at this time, left with "just-so" stories. Darwinians revert to their received wisdom: It happened, so it must have happened in a Darwinian way. (Flanagan 2009, 76–7)

However, to make mention of just-so stories at this point is really an exaggeration. Not only do we not have a credible just-so story about why evolution supposedly favored an engineering solution that produced sentience, but also we do not have a credible just-so story for how insensate life might have produced a physical entity with the capacity to experience pleasure, because no one can conceive of how the latter might be done. In the end, as Flanagan says, the Darwinian (evolutionary naturalist's) view is no more than this: "it happened, so it must have happened in a Darwinian way." After all, is there any other way in which it might have happened? Well, yes. God might have created a soul with the capacity to experience pleasure for the purpose that it experience perfect happiness, and the burden of this chapter has been to explain why there is no good reason from considerations rooted in science to think that it did not happen in this way.

Evolution versus creation

In light of the points made in the previous section, am I suggesting that evolution in the form of descent from a common ancestor did not occur? Not in the least. What I am suggesting is that this descent was constrained by the purpose for which each of us exists. My line of reasoning goes something like the following:

My purpose for existing is that I be perfectly happy. If we assume for the sake of argument that the achievement of that purpose is in some way dependent upon how I choose to live my life on this earth (see Chapter 5), then a properly functioning human body is a necessary condition for the fulfillment of that dependency condition. Could a human body that fulfills this dependency condition have evolved purposelessly? I know of no way of demonstrating that it could not have done so. But given that I exist for a purpose, it seems most plausible to hold that my body exists to enable the fulfillment of that purpose and, therefore, that the chain of descent from a common ancestor in which the human body is the latest link was ultimately purposeful in nature. Do I, then, believe that God causally intervened in the chain of descent to guide its direction? No. Do I, then, believe that God did not causally intervene in this way but prearranged things at the very beginning so that they would develop in the way that they did? No. Why can it not be the case that I simply do not know the answers to these kinds of questions (and perhaps no one else knows the answers either)? Why could it not be the case that even if the human body is ultimately designed to help promote the fulfillment of the soul's purpose for existing, it simply is not possible to read off from observations of either that body or its ancestors exactly when and where the artificer did his work, though such work was surely done? Moreover, given, as we have seen earlier in this chapter, that the argument from causal closure on behalf of naturalism fails, there is no philosophical reason to think that such work could not have been done.

Earlier in this chapter I argued that the reasoning in support of the claim that there is causal interaction between a soul and its physical body is *not* a "God-of-the-gaps" type of argument. I pointed out that, in discussions about God's existence, critics often argue that theists *postulate* God's existence in light of an inability of science to provide a complete explanation for a physical datum (or data). In light of the seemingly almost irresistible temptation that critics of theism have to make this charge, I stress that the line of reasoning put forth in the previous paragraph is also not a "God-of-the-gaps" kind of argument. My claim is *not* that there is a certain physical structure (the human body) whose existence, it is reasonable to believe, can only be explained by the purposeful causal activity of God, because science as of now has failed to find an adequate nonpurposeful physical causal story of that structure's existence. Rather, the claim is that, given that each of us has a purpose for his or her existence and that our bodies are necessary for the accomplishment of that purpose, it is reasonable to conclude that the existence of the human body is itself something that was purposed.

According to theism, then, the human body ultimately has the purpose of facilitating the fulfillment of the purpose of life, which is that a person experience perfect happiness. However, all of us are all too aware that our physical bodies are at times the source of much pain and suffering. As I pointed out in Chapter 1, Augustine took this fact to demonstrate that life's purpose could not be fulfilled this side of the grave. Pain and suffering are at the heart of the problem of evil, which historically has been taken to provide the biggest challenge to the truth of theism. The problem of evil is the subject matter of the next chapter.

Addendum

Anthony Kronman offers explanations for why our colleges and universities have given up on providing a classroom forum for discussing the meaning of life (Kronman 2007). Kronman argues that two explanations of this dismissal are (1) the transformation of colleges and universities into research institutions that prize research above teaching and (2) the ascendency of political correctness that, while it touts the virtues of diversity, is more interested in indoctrination of the party line than a serious discussion of diverse ideas.

While what Kronman says is undoubtedly true, he seems blind to the doctrine of naturalism and its implications for treatments of the meaning of life in the college classroom. If naturalism is right and there ultimately are no irreducible purposeful explanations in life, then there really cannot be a purpose for discussing the meaning of life in college classrooms. Moreover, Kronman seems unaware of naturalism's implications for his own view of life's meaning. He advocates an approach to the meaning of life that he describes as "secular humanism." As he understands it, secular humanism recognizes a plurality of values and identifiable ways of life that possess intrinsic value and maintains that each of us must purposefully and freely choose from among these values and ways of life in order to lead a meaningful life. Naturalism undermines secular humanism insofar as the former affirms the truth of determinism and the illegitimacy of appealing to purposeful explanations.

5

The problem of evil

Skeptical theism, the purpose of life, and the problem of evil

According to Ellen Charry, sixteenth-century protestants "were wary of Aristotle and scholasticism—and therefore of Aquinas. Happiness was of little interest to them. While Aquinas thought from creation, Protestants thought from the Fall" (Charry 2010, 111). My theistic understanding of life's purpose as the experience of perfect happiness is framed in terms of creation, and when I considered numerous theistic objections to this view in Chapter 3, I did not consider one that some Protestant Christian theists raise in light of the doctrine of the Fall of Adam (however, one construes this), which is recorded in the biblical book of Genesis. According to these theists, the Fall negatively impacted the cognitive capacity of human beings to such a degree that they were no longer able to know the purpose of life for them as created beings. As Alasdair MacIntyre writes, with the rise of Protestantism, the view developed that "[r]eason can supply … *no* genuine comprehension of man's true end; that the power of reason was destroyed by the fall of man. 'Si Adam integer stetisset' [If Adam had stood or remained morally upright], on Calvin's view, reason might have played the part that Aristotle assigned to it" (MacIntyre 1981, 51). The part that Aristotle assigned to reason included knowing man's *telos* or end. But Adam did not remain morally upright, and a result according to this Protestant line of thought was that unaided reason could no longer know man's true end.

Not all Protestant Christian theists, however, believe that the inability to know the purpose of life is explained by the Fall. Some maintain that with or without a fall we are ignorant about such a matter, because our cognitive capacities are too limited. In contrast with us, God is omniscient and because His knowledge so greatly exceeds our own we are left wondering what His purpose for creating us is. The same kind of position is advocated by philosophers known as *skeptical theists* in their treatment of what is traditionally termed "the problem of evil." David Hume, an eighteenth-century British philosopher, recalling the ancient Greek philosopher, Epicurus, stated the problem as follows: "Is he [God] willing to prevent evil, but not able? Then he is impotent. Is he able, but not willing? Then he is malevolent. Is he both able and willing? Whence then is evil?" (Hume 1963, 567) Skeptical theists insist that although God does have a reason (justification) for permitting evil, we do not know what this reason is. We are ignorant of it because God is God and His knowledge is so much greater than our own. Hence, we should not be surprised when we draw a blank about why it is that God allows evil.

Skeptical theists are skeptical about God's justification for permitting evil. Must skeptical theists also be skeptical about the purpose of life? From what two prominent skeptical theists have written, it would appear not. For example, Alvin Plantinga, who for decades has been the most prominent spokesperson for skeptical theism, writes "I also believe in eternal life. The precise contours of this are certainly obscure, but it includes an eternity of bliss for enormous numbers of God's creatures" (Plantinga 1996, 257). Another prominent skeptical theist, William Alston, believes that the goods of the afterlife might justify God's permission of evil and states that the goods of the afterlife include "experiencing complete felicity in the everlasting presence of God" (Alston 1996a, 324). So while Plantinga and Alston do not explicitly state that experiencing perfect happiness is the purpose of life, their comments about eternal bliss and complete felicity seem to imply an implicit affirmation of this view on their part.

But appearances can be deceiving. Perhaps skeptical theists like Plantinga and Alston might affirm that a person's greatest good is perfect happiness but insist that they do not know if experiencing perfect happiness is the (or even a) purpose for which God creates us. Perhaps they would affirm no more than that having a reasonable opportunity to experience perfect happiness is a necessary condition of (requirement for) whatever God's creative purpose for us is.

While I know of no way of showing that a position like the one just described, which distinguishes between experiencing perfect happiness and the purpose of life, is false, the distinction seems to be of no real consequence for our own greatest good and, therefore, the making of it lacks motivation and begs for an explanation. This is the case, for three reasons.

First, given that it seems to us that experiencing perfect happiness is the purpose of life, a skeptical theist who claims not to know that experiencing perfect happiness is life's purpose raises questions about the plausibility of his version of theism. Second, a skeptical theist, about whether experiencing perfect happiness is life's purpose, *knows* that perfect happiness is a person's greatest good and that God must ensure the possibility of reasonably achieving this good, whatever the purpose is for which He creates human beings. This knowledge is significant in its own right and makes clear that a skeptical theist's skepticism about the purpose of life is significantly qualified. Third, what is of most interest to me is my own greatest good (and, I assume, others are like me in being most interested in their own greatest good), and so long as the possibility of achieving that good is reasonably available to me, the question about what God's reason for creating me is, assuming for the sake of discussion that this reason is different from my experiencing my greatest good, ceases to be of any serious concern to me. Given that God's purpose for creating me, whatever it is, must be consistent with me having a reasonable opportunity of experiencing my greatest good (which all reasonable theists, including skeptical theists, will concede), it seems that there is no good reason to affirm that the purpose of life is something other than experiencing perfect happiness and, therefore, it is reasonable to conclude that the experience of my greatest good just is the purpose for which God created me.

Now, if it is difficult to make a convincing case for a skeptical theistic position regarding the purpose of life, might it not be just as difficult to make a convincing case for a skeptical theistic position concerning God's justification for allowing evil? I believe that the answer to this question is "Yes," because I believe knowledge of the purpose of life provides insight into God's reason for allowing evil. In other words, I believe that knowledge of the purpose of life aids in the construction of a theodicy, where a theodicy (from the Greek

words *theos*, which means "God" and *dikē*, which means "justice")
is an explanation, at least in part, of God's reason for allowing evil.
Before arguing for this position, however, I turn in the next two
sections to a discussion of the idea of choosing a life plan and its
relation to perfect happiness, which will aid me in my subsequent
development of a theodicy.

Choice and life plans

To recap briefly some points that I made about goodness in earlier
chapters, it is important to remember that "good" is a value term
whose most fundamental instances are nonmoral in nature and
come in the form of experiences of pleasure. Thus, a life of nothing
but pleasure is good for each of us in the sense that it maximizes our
well-being. Indeed, this kind of life is our supreme good. However,
not only is our highest good the experience of perfect happiness,
but in addition we, in light of our self-consciousness, are aware that
this is the case. What is also true of us is that we are aware that we
are beings who persist through time as the same selves or persons.
This is not to say that we do not change at all. We do. For example,
our characters and interests often change over time. But we well
understand that a person who was, say, angry and bitter years ago,
can now be at peace with himself or herself and the world, while
remaining the same self or person through this change.

In light of our awareness of ourselves as beings that persist
self-identical through time, we come to understand the necessity
of making plans about our future actions. Our designations of
ourselves as spouses, teachers, truck drivers, and professional
athletes convey an implicit recognition on our part that we follow
regular patterns of behavior as the result of making plans. Thus,
as a teacher, I am cognizant of my duties to my students and arise
every day with a fairly regular routine of going to class, grading,
researching, and writing already planned out. The same truth about
plans applies to a professional athlete who practices, travels, and
plays games according to a schedule. As the philosopher Michael
Bratman has made clear (Bratman 1987), we are planning agents
who choose and, thereby, form intentions in advance about more or
less complex plans concerning our futures, where these plans guide
our later actions. In the words of Thomas Nagel, "[n]ot only are

[peoples'] lives full of particular choices that hang together in larger activities with temporal structure: they also decide in the broadest terms what to pursue and what to avoid, what the priorities among their various aims should be, and what kind of people they want to be or become" (Nagel 1979, 14). According to Robert Nozick, our broadest or most expansive intentions are *life plans*:

> To intend that my life be a certain way, I must have an intention ... that focuses upon my life as a whole .... The strongest sort of intention about one's life is a *life plan*, an individual's set of coherent, systematic purposes and intentions for his life.... A life plan specifies the intentional focus of a person's life, his major goals (perhaps partially ordering them), his conception of himself, his purposes, what if anything he dedicates or devotes himself to, and so forth.... [A] life plan focuses on a person's whole life or a significant chunk of it as a life. (Nozick 1981, 577)

If we combine the insights of Bratman, Nagel, and Nozick, we end up with the idea that we choose and, thereby, settle on life plans by making what we can plausibly think of as *self*-forming choices (SFCs) (Kane 1996, Chapter 8). Thus, I chose to form my self into a spouse, father, teacher, and writer, while others have chosen to form themselves in both similar and different ways. As I have already emphasized, these kinds of choices introduce a significant degree of regular behavior into our daily lives, with different SFCs introducing different kinds of regular behavior.

Before proceeding, it is necessary to dispose of one possible objection to the idea that we make SFCs. In a skeptical vein about the reality of SFCs, the philosopher and atheist Daniel Dennett suggests that we pause to ask just how often we make SFCs: "Once a day on average, or once a year or once a decade? Do they tend to start at birth, at age five, at puberty?" (Dennett 2003, 127) Now, if SFCs really are plans about our behavior patterns over substantive periods of time, it should be obvious that we do not make them all that often. For example, none of us makes a career choice every day. Rather, we choose a career and then settle down into a pattern of regular activity. While making a career choice does not entail that one will never change one's mind about one's future career endeavors, it does ensure that one will not be changing one's mind about a career every other day. Dennett has been a philosophy professor for decades, which is evidence that he was not making career choices on average once a day or even once a decade.

Though SFCs concerning marriage, parenthood, and careers are broad in terms of their scope of influence over the activities that are carried out by us in our daily lives, I think it is plausible to maintain that none of them is the most wide-ranging or important SFC that an individual makes. Each of these SFCs is itself nested within an even wider-ranging SFC. Most importantly, and in light of the points made in previous chapters about happiness and its goodness, I think a reasonable case can be developed for the view that an agent's most broadly influential SFC is about *when* he will maximize his happiness and *how*, where the how consists of the kind of life plan he will adopt in pursuit of that happiness. Because happiness is intrinsically good, I will term this most wide-ranging SFC a *good-seeking* SFC. The following quote from Owen Flanagan about a choice of St Augustine's nicely illustrates the kind of SFC that I have in mind:

> St. Augustine was the ultimate party animal until his early thirties, at which point he changed his ways and became an exemplary moral person, a great philosopher, a bishop, and eventually a saint. We might say that Augustine was ruled by his passions until he saw the light in his early thirties. But according to [our conception of free will], we would not mean that he *couldn't* control himself. We would mean that he chose not to control himself or chose to control himself badly [when he could have chosen to control himself or to control himself well]. (Flanagan 2002, 58)

What Flanagan is suggesting about Augustine is something like the following. At a certain point in his life, Augustine made a free, in the sense of not being determined, good-seeking SFC that entailed he would not restrain himself from pursuing certain means to maximizing his immediate or short-term happiness. Then, some years later, he made a different good-seeking SFC that entailed he would restrain his pursuit of goods that promoted his short-term happiness, where exercising this restraint involved his planned avoidance of performing certain kinds of actions. Augustine's own account of this latter good-seeking SFC supports Flanagan's description of it. While Augustine says he was converted to God in whom he believed he would find long-term, perfect happiness, it is clear from his summary of the events leading up to that conversion that he understood that this good-seeking SFC entailed that he would purposefully no longer seek to satisfy desires that had lured him into theft, sexual promiscuity, etc., and the promotion of his short-term happiness:

> But now ... as I heard how [two men] had made the choice that was to save them by giving themselves up entirely to your [God's] care, the more bitterly I hated myself in comparison with them.... [N]o more was required than an act of will. But it must be a resolute and whole-hearted act of the will .... I was held back by mere trifles, the most paltry inanities, all my old attachments. They plucked at my garment of flesh and whispered, "Are you going to dismiss us? From this moment we shall never be with you again, for ever and ever. From this moment you will never again be allowed to do this thing or that, for evermore." (Augustine 1961, VIII, 7, 8, 11)

It is plausible, then, to understand Augustine's conversion as a good-seeking SFC in which he chose a life plan that he believed would maximize his later experience of happiness (this belief, which is implicit in Augustine's comment that the choice of the two men would save them, will be made explicit a few paragraphs hence), where that choice entailed a commitment on his part to restrain himself from pursuing his short-term happiness in certain ways. Now restraint includes taking positive steps to avoid future situations wherein one would likely experience temptation to enjoy one's old attachments. For example, I have a good friend who was formerly an alcoholic. As he became more and more enslaved to the bottle, he alienated his family members and found it impossible to keep a job. As he explained to me, he had to make a choice and the choice on his part to "dry out" entailed that he plan not to socialize with certain people, that he not frequent old haunts, that he not have any alcohol in his home, etc. Of course, as many of us were taught in our youth, our best-laid plans sometimes are not good enough. Thus, even though my friend took every precaution to avoid socializing with certain people, etc., there was (and is) always the chance of his meeting those individuals at a place where he would least expect to do so. Were that to occur, he might be invited to go to some place with them and would have to make a choice about whether or not to accept the invitation. In essence, a good-seeking SFC like that made by Augustine is a means to reducing the need to make certain future choices. In the case of my friend, were his best-laid plans successful, he would effectively eliminate the need to make future choices in the face of certain temptations, because he made plans to avoid altogether situations in which those temptations might arise. Such a good-seeking SFC entails a plan to minimize the need to make certain choices in the future.

Though Augustine's good-seeking SFC involved a conversion to Christianity, there is nothing essentially Christian about the idea of a good-seeking SFC that requires restrained pursuit of short-term happiness. This is because all of us as individual human beings, whether Christian or not, have a desire for our own short-term happiness. Given our desire for our own happiness in the short term, we have a reason to act for the sake of our own immediate well-being. However, because we also believe that other persons exist who share this desire for their own short-term happiness, in certain circumstances we believe that were we to act in certain ways we would undermine their opportunity to satisfy their desire for their own short-term well-being, an opportunity to which they have as much right as we have to our own. As a result of what we believe about the potential impact of our actions on the immediate well-being of others, we come to have moral beliefs about certain kinds of actions that we should not perform. The upshot of this line of reasoning is that we come to possess beliefs about permissible and impermissible ways of pursuing what we believe is good and will promote our short-term happiness, where we view the former ways of pursuing what is good as *just* (moral) and the latter ways as *unjust* (immoral). Given these ideas about just and unjust ways of pursuing what is good, we form ideas about two corresponding life plans, one which consists of restraint in the pursuit of what conduces to our short-term happiness and the other which does not. A good-seeking choice of the former kind of life plan, which is the kind that Augustine made in his early thirties, is what I will call a *just*-good-seeking SFC, while a good-seeking choice of the latter way of life is what I will term an *unjust*-good-seeking SFC. In simplest terms, a just-good-seeking SFC is a choice to live a life of restraint in pursuit of what is good, while an unjust-good-seeking SFC is a choice not to exercise this restraint. An unjust-good-seeking SFC is essentially a choice to reserve the right in any situation to pursue happiness against the dictates of conscience. With a just-good-seeking SFC, one does not presume the right to pursue what is good in whatever way one wants. And when one fails for whatever reason to follow through on one's just-good-seeking SFC (e.g. the former alcoholic succumbs to the temptation for a drink in a situation where he believed there was no risk that alcohol would be served), then one asks for forgiveness of whomever one has wronged. This is because a just-good-seeking SFC is, among other things, a commitment to ask for forgiveness in the future whenever it is necessary to do so.

At this juncture, it might be argued that while no one can be mistaken about the intrinsic goodness of pleasure and the intrinsic evilness of pain, what a person believes about permissible and impermissible ways of pursuing and avoiding this good and evil, respectively, could be erroneous. In other words, what a person subjectively regards as either just or unjust might not be objectively so. Hence, it is possible for a person to choose a life plan that he or she believes (subjectively) is just when in reality (objectively) it is (in whole or in part) unjust.

While the distinction referred to in this objection is a real one, it is not relevant to the issue at hand. What is relevant is the fact that people make a just- or an unjust-good-seeking SFC in light of their beliefs about what is just and unjust, regardless of whether those beliefs are true or false, and they understand that they are obligated to make a just-good-seeking SFC in light of those beliefs by virtue of their conscience, where their conscience is an inner voice that pronounces a verdict of innocence or guilt upon them depending on whether they make a just- or an unjust-good-seeking SFC. The Christian apostle St Paul frequently appealed to this notion of conscience, as in the following comments in his Letter to the Romans 2: 14–5: "When Gentiles who have not the law do by nature what the law requires, they are a law to themselves, even though they do not have the law. They show that what the law requires is written on their hearts, while their conscience also bears witness and their conflicting thoughts accuse or perhaps excuse them ...." The philosopher Immanuel Kant also recognized the importance of conscience:

[T]he accusation of conscience cannot be ... readily dismissed, neither should it be; it is not a matter of the will .... Conscience is an instinct to judge with legal authority according to moral laws; it pronounces a judicial verdict, and, like a judge who can only punish or acquit but cannot reward, so also our conscience either acquits or declares us guilty and deserving of punishment. (Kant 1963, 131)

The concept of a conscience proves useful when considering the matter of who does and who does not deserve to experience perfect happiness, which is the topic I address in the next section.

Life plans and perfect happiness

It is now time to tie the idea of life plans and just- and unjust-good-seeking SFCs to the matter of perfect happiness. The link is as follows: those who make a just-good-seeking choice are plumping for a way of life that will result in maximizing their long-term happiness (in the form of perfect happiness), while those who make an unjust-good-seeking choice are plumping for maximizing their short-term happiness at the expense of forfeiting perfect happiness. In simplest terms, ultimate justice is the idea of a separation of persons on the basis of their ultimate choices about life plans into two modes of existence. Perfect happiness will be experienced by those who have made a just-good-seeking choice of a way of life and it will not be experienced by those who have made an unjust-good-seeking choice of a way of life. Thus, the matter of who will and who will not experience perfect happiness must ultimately be understood in terms of how a person chooses to live his or her life in pursuit of what is good. Does an individual choose a way of life of restraint and deference to others who are created by God in the short term with the result that he or she will experience perfect happiness in the long term? Or does a person choose a way of life of a lack of restraint and deference to others for the purpose of maximizing his or her own happiness in the short term at the expense of not experiencing perfect happiness in the long term?

   At its heart, then, a just-good-seeking SFC is a choice to renounce trying to experience in the short run as much happiness as possible on one's own unjust terms and to trust God to grant perfect happiness in the end as a result of one's having led a life of restraint in pursuit of happiness right now. Thus, happiness and morality ultimately meet and embrace in a just-good-seeking choice whose content concerns trusting God for the provision of perfect happiness and whose purpose is that one do what is morally right. Stated slightly differently, a just-good-seeking SFC is a choice to trust God (to acknowledge his existence and worship Him) for the maximization of one's happiness, where God is analogous to Nozick's hypothetical experience machine. What the idea of the experience machine gets right, beyond the fact that perfect happiness consists of experiencing nothing but pleasure, is the fact that the fulfillment of one's purpose for existing, while contingent upon one making the right kind of SFC, is ultimately something with respect to which one is passive. One chooses to trust and, thereby, admits one's ultimate dependence upon God for the experience of the perfect happiness for which one was created.

The making of a just-good-seeking SFC also has social impli-cations. Those who make such a choice know all too well the barrier that it creates with others who make an unjust-good-seeking SFC. Those who make the former choice are routinely thought of by those who make the latter choice as boring, prudes, goodie-goodies, etc., because the former refuse to share in some of the good-seeking activities of the latter. Given that the members of the one group make a different good-seeking SFC than the members of the latter, members of each prefer to go their separate ways in their pursuit of happiness. Thus, in the afterlife, God will ultimately separate the two groups. As C. S. Lewis writes:

> Either the day must come when joy prevails and all the makers of misery are no longer able to infect it: or else for ever and ever the makers of misery can destroy in others the happiness they reject for themselves. (Lewis 2001b, 136)

> [T]he damned are, in one sense, successful, rebels to the end; that the doors of hell are locked on the *inside*.... In the long run the answer to all those who object to the doctrine of hell, is itself a question: "What are you asking God to do?" To wipe out their past sins and, at all costs, to give them a fresh start, smoothing every difficulty and offering every miraculous help? But He has done so, on Calvary. To forgive them? They will not be forgiven. To leave them alone? Alas, I am afraid that is what He does. (Lewis 1962, 127–8)

> There are only two kinds of people in the end: those who say to God, "Thy will be done," and those to whom God says, in the end, "Thy will be done." (Lewis 2001b, 75)

In terms of conscience, the point of this section is that there are only two kinds of people in the end: those who choose as a way of life to follow the dictates of their conscience and trust God (or whatever occupies the role of God in their belief system) for the fulfillment of their desire for perfect happiness and those who choose as a way of life not to follow those dictates and not to trust God. The former is a just-good-seeking SFC and the latter is an unjust-good-seeking SFC. These two kinds of SFCs are not defined in terms of the contents of consciences, which can vary from person to person. But two people whose consciences differ in content to one degree or another can both make the same just- or unjust-good-seeking SFC. Those who make a just-good-seeking SFC want to end up being with others who make the same choice, while those who make an unjust-good-seeking SFC desire not to be with those who make just-good-seeking SFCs. The former will in the end experience the perfect happiness for which they were created. The latter will not.

Lewis captures this point about the role of conscience in just- and unjust-good-seeking SFCs in *The Last Battle*, which is the final book in his Narnia series. Emeth, who was an unwitting follower of the evil god, Tash, is in the end welcomed by the Christ-like lion, Aslan, on the basis of Emeth's adherence to conscience:

> Then I fell at his feet and thought, Surely this is the hour of death, for the Lion (who is worthy of all honor) will know that I have served Tash all my days and not him.... But the Glorious One bent down his golden head and touched my forehead with his tongue and said, Son, thou art welcome. But I said, Alas, Lord, I am no son of thine but the servant of Tash. He answered, Child, all the service thou hast done to Tash, I account as service done to me.... But I said also (for the truth constrained me), Yet I have been seeking Tash all my days. Beloved, said the Glorious One, unless thy desire had been for me thou wouldst not have sought so long and so truly. For all find what they truly seek. (Lewis 1984, 204–6)

Emeth, believing erroneously through no fault of his own that Tash was the true God, obeyed his conscience and served Tash. Given his obedience to what he believed was true and just, Aslan welcomed Emeth because he had made a just-good-seeking SFC.

In developing my position on who does and who does not deserve perfect happiness, I have been implicitly assuming that the person who makes a good-seeking SFC believes that our world is meaningful in the sense that things ultimately fit together in an intelligible way (see Question 3 in Chapter 1). What if, however, a person is a Russellian (see Chapter 2) who maintains that the world is ultimately absurd, at least in terms of morality and self-interest ultimately failing to embrace, but nevertheless makes a just-good-seeking SFC? Does this individual deserve to be rewarded with perfect happiness?

If one is considering the issue of consistency among one's assertions, then the following response from God would be in keeping with the Russellian world view: "To you according to your belief, and given that you believe our world is ultimately absurd in terms of morality and self-interest failing to embrace, there is no reason why your just-good-seeking SFC should be rewarded with perfect happiness." But might this position be inconsistent with my endorsement of conscience as expressed in Lewis' story about Emeth and Tash? After all, if through no fault of his own Emeth believed that Tash was Aslan (the one true God) and was rewarded for his just-good-seeking SFC, then perhaps through no fault of his own a Russellian believes the world is absurd and yet makes a just-good-seeking SFC that is in accordance with his conscience. And if this is the case, then would it not be right for God to reward him with perfect happiness for his choice?

There is, however, a problem with likening a Russellian with the above-stated belief about the absurd nature of the world to Emeth with his belief about Tash. The problem is that a typical Russellian believes much more than that the world is ultimately absurd. For example, a Russellian routinely embraces the naturalist belief that everything that happens in the world can ultimately be explained without any mention of a purpose (see Chapter 4). Moreover, given this belief about the nonexistence of ultimate purposeful explanation, a naturalist denies that we make any undetermined choices that are ultimately explained by purposes. The upshot is that given the truth of what a Russellian believes about the nonexistence of purposeful explanation and the fact that one can only (try to) do what one believes is not impossible to do, a Russellian cannot make a just-good-seeking SFC because such a choice, if it occurs, is an undetermined event that is ultimately explained by a purpose.

Given that a Russellian cannot make such a choice he cannot be rewarded with perfect happiness for making it.

A theodicy

By way of summary, then, people desire the happiness that by nature constitutes their well-being and in its perfect form is their ultimate purpose. Given this human nature, they must make a good-seeking SFC that is concerned with *when* and *how* they will maximize the happiness that they cannot help but desire to experience. A just-good-seeking SFC will lead to the experience of perfect happiness in the afterlife, while an unjust-good-seeking SFC will preclude the experience of that happiness in the afterlife.

Given our human nature, we all desire happiness and must make a choice in the form of a good-seeking SFC about when and how we will pursue it. However, the problem of evil reminds us that no matter what kind of good-seeking SFC we make in this life, whether just or unjust, we are vulnerable to experiencing evil. I quote again (see Chapter 1) Augustine's description of the nature of this world:

> As for those who have supposed that the sovereign good [is] to be found in this life, and have placed it either in the soul or the body, or in both, or, to speak more explicitly, either in pleasure or in virtue, or in both; in repose or in virtue, or in both; in pleasure and repose, or in virtue, or in all combined; in the primary objects of nature, or in virtue, or in both,—all these have, with a marvelous shallowness, sought to find their blessedness in this life and in themselves. Contempt has been poured upon such ideas by the Truth....
>
> For what flood of eloquence can suffice to detail the miseries of this life? ... Is the body of the wise man exempt from any pain which may dispel pleasure, from any disquietude which may banish repose? The amputation or decay of the members of the body puts an end to its integrity, deformity blights its beauty, weakness its health, lassitude its vigour, sleepiness or sluggishness its activity,–and which of these is it that may not assail the flesh of the wise man? Comely and fitting attitudes and movements of the body are numbered among the prime natural blessings; but what if some sickness makes the members

tremble? What if a man suffers from curvature of the spine to such an extent that his hands reach the ground, and he goes upon all-fours like a quadruped? ... but what kind of sense is it that remains when a man becomes deaf and blind? Where are reason and intellect when disease makes a man delirious? (Augustine 1993, xix. 4)

Confident that perfect happiness is a person's greatest good and certain that it cannot be had in this life, Augustine concluded that if perfect happiness is to be had at all, it must be had in the afterlife (Augustine 1993, xix.10). Consider, now, a simple thought experiment that is proposed by the philosopher Michael Slote about two kinds of lives, one that starts out well and ends poorly, and the other that starts out poorly and ends well:

A given man may achieve political power and, once in power, do things of great value, after having been in the political wilderness throughout his earlier career. He may later die while still "in harness" and fully possessed of his powers, at a decent old age. By contrast, another man may have a meteoric success in youth, attaining the same office as the first man and also achieving much good; but then lose power, while still young, never to regain it. Without hearing anything more, I think our natural, immediate reaction to these examples would be that the first man was the more fortunate, and this seems to express a preference for goods that come late in life. (Slote 1983, 23–4)

It seems to me that Slote is undoubtedly correct about our natural judgment concerning the lives of the two men (I explain why he is correct below). On the assumption that he is right, I am going to take his idea about our preference for goods that come late in life and combine it with both the idea of perfect happiness in the afterlife as an individual's ultimate good and the idea of a just-good-seeking SFC, and use all three ideas to develop a theodicy. I will develop this theodicy from within the Christian tradition because, as I stated in the preface to this book, the Christian religious tradition is the one with which I am most familiar. However, I stress that my theodicy is not Christian in the sense that its philosophical content cannot be found in any other religion. Indeed, I would be highly surprised if that were the case.

According to Slote, when presented with the two lives just sketched, we prefer the one in which the goods come later rather than earlier in life. Slote believes that at least a partial explanation of this preference is our belief "that what happens early in life can be compensated for by what happens later" (Slote 1983, 26). This seems right and according to theism perfect happiness is what happens later in life to perform this compensatory and redemptive function. Moreover, perfect happiness is qualified to perform this function because it is without end and, thereby, could not be reversed by subsequent experiences of evil.

If Slote is right, an atheist, like anyone else, does not have a problem with the idea of a later good redeeming an earlier evil. In two insightful papers, Joshua Seachris argues that the question "What is the meaning of life?" is best understood in terms of a narrative about issues such as life's purpose and what makes life worth living (Seachris 2009, 2011). In terms of questions (1)–(3) from the outset of Chapter 1, Seachris believes "What is the meaning of life?" is best understood in terms of a narrative about a person's life that fits things together in an intelligible way (question (3)) through the concepts of purpose (question (1)) and what makes life worth living (question (2)). Echoing Slote's point about what comes later in life redeeming what comes earlier, Seachris stresses that the ending of a narrative of a person's life is of paramount importance for evaluating that life as a whole and whether it is futile (absurd) or not. There are, says Seachris, at least three ways of understanding the concept of an ending of life:

> (i) ending as *termination*, (ii) ending as *telos*, and (iii) ending as *closure*. The first sense of ending is that of something being *finished*. Locutions such as "the race is over", or "I am finished with school", or "it ceased to exist", all capture important connotations of this sense of ending. The second sense of ending tracks the notion of … purpose…. Importantly, ending as telos … carries additional connotations of … the purposeful progression of the plot within a narrative toward an intended end. Finally, the third sense of ending, ending as closure, refers to a contextually anchored settled stance with respect to a "problem" or cluster of problems emerging within a given narrative or portion of that narrative.

These three senses of ending differ conceptually, though they are compatible. (Seachris 2011, 148)

Perfect happiness is an ending in each of the senses (i)–(iii). It is (i) the finishing of a life because (ii) it is the achievement of the purpose for which a person is created by God. And, as I will argue in the rest of this chapter, perfect happiness as an end provides (iii) closure because it is the central idea in the explanation for why God allows us to experience evil. In Seachris' words, "[g]enerally, it is thought by theists that, in some sense, the blessed final state is part of a fuller answer to the problem of evil.... The very general and modest claim I am advocating is simply that, given ... the *nature* of a given ending, some measure of plausibility is brought to the practice of enlisting eschatological considerations in the [project of] theodicy" (Seachris 2011, 158). Given the central importance of the nature of an ending of a person's life for dealing with the problem of evil, the theodicy that I will defend is as follows: Perfect happiness is a great *good*. Indeed, it is the *greatest* good that a person might experience. Because it is the greatest good that an individual might experience, not just anyone *deserves* to experience it. Only those who make a just-good-seeking SFC deserve perfect happiness. Thus, in order for God to grant perfect happiness in a just way, he must give human beings the opportunity to make an undetermined choice about which kind of good-seeking life plan they will pursue. However, to allow human beings to have this kind of freedom of choice entails allowing them to make an unjust-good-seeking SFC, which results in the production of pain in the world. What justifies God allowing human beings to experience evil, then, is the need to give them the freedom to make an undetermined choice of either a just- or unjust-good-seeking SFC. And God must give human beings this kind of freedom because not just anyone deserves to experience the greatest good of perfect happiness. Because the just experience of perfect happiness is conditional in nature—people will experience perfect happiness if and only if they choose justly (they make a just-good-seeking SFC)—I will sometimes say that a justification for God's allowing evil is that people have the possibility of experiencing perfect happiness. So while the purpose for which a person exists is that he or she experience perfect happiness, God's justification for allowing the experience of evil is that a person *justly* experiences the perfect happiness for which he or she is created. Thus, the requirement of justice entails that each person must make a choice in the form of a good-seeking SFC that will determine whether he or she fulfills the purpose for which he or she exists.

In an effort to avoid any confusion about the role of freedom of choice (free will) in my proposed theodicy, it is important to emphasize that while God's justification for allowing evil requires that human beings have free will (as I will use it throughout this chapter, "free will" means the power to make undetermined choices), that they possess this freedom is not God's justification for permitting evil. Free will cannot occupy this justificatory role because it is not an intrinsic good. It is no more than an instrumental good, the possession of which by persons is necessary for their justly experiencing the perfect happiness that constitutes the fulfillment of the purpose for which they are created by God.

The plausibility of my theodicy

As a way of elucidating the plausibility of the theodicy that I am proposing, it is helpful to reintroduce skeptical theism (see the opening section of this chapter) and consider the following scenario: Assume that one is a skeptical theist who, by definition, claims not to know what God's justification for allowing evil is. Though one does not know what God's justification for permitting evil is, one knows that there is (because there must be) a justification. Now also assume that while one knows that there is a justification, one is informed that, whatever that justification is, it is compatible with no one ever experiencing perfect happiness, regardless of the choices they make in this life, even the making of a just-good-seeking SFC. What should one say about this scenario?

If one is a reasonable skeptical theist who acknowledges that experiencing perfect happiness is the purpose of life, then it seems that one must deny that this scenario is possible. After all, one knows that God's purpose for creating persons is that they experience perfect happiness and for Him not to allow for the achievement of this purpose, no matter what choice a person might make, is absurd. Given this knowledge of God's purpose for creating persons and the fact that they must have the free will that makes possible not only the experience of this perfect happiness but also the existence of evil, it seems that in light of the argument of the previous section, skeptical theists do know why God allows evil.

In an effort to avoid affirming what I have argued in the previous two paragraphs while nevertheless conceding some knowledge of why God allows evil, a skeptical theist might insist that the knowledge he or she possesses is no more than knowledge of the reasons God does not have for justifying His permission of evil. For example, a skeptical theist might affirm that God does not allow despots to rob, torture, and rape those whom they oppress for the purpose that they (the despots) experience perfect happiness as a reward for their actions. Beyond knowing this, however, a skeptical theist might maintain ignorance about what God's reason for permitting evil is.

I believe that this kind of minimalist epistemic position is implausible. To see why, consider another scenario similar to the one just outlined. In this scenario, a skeptical theist not only continues to affirm knowledge of reasons God does not have for allowing evil but also insists that any reason God has for permitting evil is compatible with created persons, for reasons that have absolutely nothing to do with how they choose, either (1) spending an eternity in hell (for the sake of discussion, I will assume that hell is an existence with more than its fair share of pain), (2) spending a finite period of time in hell after which they are annihilated, or (3) being annihilated at death (there is no afterlife of any kind). It seems that no reasonable skeptical theist would affirm that God's justification for allowing evil is compatible with one or more of these three alternatives. But why would no reasonable skeptical theist affirm this compatibility? The most plausible answer is that he or she knows that God's justification for permitting evil includes the purpose that created persons have the possibility of experiencing perfect happiness, where the free choice involved in having the possibility makes possible unjust choices that produce evil.

At this point in the argument, a skeptical theist might concede that while it is not possible for God to justify the permission of evil under any scenario like (1), (2), or (3), nevertheless, it still does not follow that he or she knows God's justification for allowing evil. This is because it might be the case that an experience of perfect happiness, for whatever reason, is not possible (e.g. the idea of perfect happiness is itself incoherent).

Even if this were the case (though, as I have already pointed out, skeptical theists such as Plantinga and Alston do believe that perfect happiness is possible), it would still be the case that a reasonable skeptical theist would have to concede knowledge of God's justification for allowing evil. This is because the gist of my argument is as follows: In order for a skeptical theist not to concede knowledge of God's reason for permitting evil, he or she must refuse to acknowledge the impossibility of a scenario in which there is a possible justification for permitting evil and it is the case that no person with free will will experience the greatest possible happiness that can be experienced, regardless of the kinds of choices that he or she makes in this life. That is, even if perfect happiness is not the greatest happiness that a person might experience, then whatever that greatest possible happiness is, a skeptical theist can reasonably deny knowledge of God's justification for permitting evil, which is specified in terms of that happiness and free will, only by refusing to acknowledge the impossibility of scenarios like (1) through (3).

As I highlighted in the opening section of this chapter, William Alston is a skeptical theist who discusses the idea of perfect happiness. According to Alston, Christian theism claims that

one's life on earth is only a tiny proportion of one's total life span…. [W]hy suppose that we are entitled to judge that justifying goods, if any, would be realized during the sufferer's earthly life, unless we have specific reasons to the contrary? … Why is the burden of proof on the suggestion of the realization of the goods in an afterlife? (Alston 1996b, 104, 123, endnote 17)

What is significant for present purposes is that Alston holds that the goods of the afterlife include "experiencing complete felicity in the everlasting presence of God" (Alston 1996a, 324). Nevertheless, he adds that the problem for constructing a theodicy is that the goods of the afterlife are of a kind of which we have no experience and only a slight grasp of their value (Alston 1996a, 324). As a result, he says "we are in a bad position to determine whether the magnitude of [complete felicity in the everlasting presence of God] is such as to make it worthwhile for God to permit a certain evil in order to make its realization possible" (Alston 1996a, 324).

Two matters are now worth consideration. First, are we really in as bad a position as Alston suggests about knowing whether an individual's perfect happiness is a good of such a nature as to justify God's permission of evil? After all, if that which constitutes a person's well-being, which perfect happiness does, is not such a good, then what might be such a good? As the philosopher William Rowe states:

[I]t is reasonable to believe that the goods for the sake of which [God] permits much intense human suffering are goods that either are or include good experiences of the humans that endure the suffering. I say this because we normally would not regard someone as morally justified in permitting intense, involuntary suffering on the part of another, if that other were not to figure significantly in the good for which that suffering was necessary. We have reason to believe, then, that the goods for the sake of which much human suffering is permitted will include conscious experiences of these humans, conscious experiences that are themselves good.... So if such goods do occur we are likely to know them. (Rowe 1986, 244)

The reasonable thing to add to Rowe's thoughts at this point is that we do know these goods. They are experiences of pleasure which are such that, when combined with the complete absence of experiences of pain, constitute the perfect happiness that is the well-being that human beings were created to experience.

Second, what begs for an answer is the question of how Alston would respond to the scenario where evils experienced by human beings have a justification, but it is the case that no individual will experience perfect happiness, even if that person makes the required just-good-seeking SFC. If Alston is right and we do not have an adequate grasp of what constitutes our own well-being and complete felicity in God's presence, then it seems that he could not rule out the possibility of this scenario in a world created by God. However, if Alston were to insist that this scenario is impossible, then what better explanation could there be for his ruling it out than that he does know the value of perfect happiness for a human being and that God's justification for allowing evil is the purpose that a person have the possibility of experiencing perfect happiness?

Not so fast!

Perhaps, however, I have moved too quickly. After all, even if it is true that the likes of Alston (and Plantinga) would deny the possibility of the scenarios that I have proposed, is it not still open to them as skeptical theists to maintain that the possibility of experiencing perfect happiness, while a necessary condition of (requirement for) whatever is God's justification for allowing evil, is no more than a necessary condition of that justification, where that justification remains beyond our intellectual ken? Alston seems to adopt this kind of "halfway house" position. After proposing some justifications that God might have for permitting evil (but which we do not know are His justifications), Alston says the following:

> [A] perfectly good God would not wholly sacrifice the welfare of one of His intelligent creatures simply in order to achieve a good for others, or for Himself. This would be incompatible with His concern for the welfare of each of His creatures. Any plan that God could implement will include provision for each of us having a life that is, on balance, a good thing, and one in which the person reaches the point of being able to see that his life as a whole is a good for him. Or at least, where free creaturely responses have a significant bearing on the overall quality of the person's life, any possible divine plan will have to provide for each of us to have the chance (or perhaps many chances) for such an outcome, if our free responses are of the right sort. (Alston 1996b, 111)

I do not know of a way to decisively rebut a position like Alston's that seems to distinguish between God's justification for allowing evil and the possibility of experiencing perfect happiness, where the latter is no more than a necessary condition of the former. However, this distinction seems contrived and of no real consequence. Therefore, the making of it begs for an explanation. This is so, for two reasons.

First, Alston's "halfway house" position concedes the following *knowledge* about what justifies God's permission of evil: we know that God cannot sacrifice the perfect happiness of a created person regardless of how that person uses his or her free will, for the sake of a justification that He has for allowing evil. This is substantive knowledge in its own right, which is analogous to knowing that perfect happiness is a person's greatest good while claiming not to know whether it is life's purpose. Second, given that Alston's skeptical theistic position is that God's allowing me (or anyone else) to experience evil is justified only if He has the purpose of granting me the possibility of experiencing perfect happiness, a natural question to ask is "Why is the latter a necessary condition of the former?" The most plausible answer is that without the latter, the allowance of the experience of evil would not be justified. In other words, the purpose of granting the possibility of experiencing perfect happiness is a necessary condition of God's allowing the experience of evil only because it *justifies* that allowance. Moreover, because purposefully granting the possibility of experiencing perfect happiness requires allowing for the exercise of free will and the making of unjust-good-seeking choices, it provides an explanation for the occurrence of experiences of evil. So it is only plausible to conclude that the divine purpose that justifies allowing me (and others) to experience evil just is the purpose that I have the possibility of experiencing perfect happiness.

A skeptical theist turned theodicist

Though for years the most prominent skeptical theist, Plantinga has recently embraced a theodicy (Plantinga 2004). According to his theodicy, God's justificatory purpose for allowing created persons to experience evil is that, through the life and death of Christ, the great goods of incarnation (God taking on a human body) and atonement be instantiated. Plantinga is careful to make clear that atonement, which presupposes incarnation, is a matter of created persons being saved from the consequences of their sin (their morally wrong or unjust choices). Thus, if there were no morally unjust choices and the pain and suffering that come with them, there could and would not be any atonement. Morally unjust choices and pain and suffering are necessary conditions of atonement, and because God wanted to create a world with a certain level of goodness, and every world with that or a greater level of goodness contains incarnation and atonement, our world had to include evil.

Plantinga considers various objections to his theodicy. In order to clarify the theodicy that I have proposed, it is most helpful to consider Plantinga's response to what he terms the "Munchausen Syndrome by Proxy." The Munchausen Syndrome describes parents who mistreat or abuse their children for the purpose that they (the parents) act virtuously and save their children from their mistreatment and abuse. Does not Plantinga's theodicy describe a divine parent who mistreats his children by creating them for the purpose that they choose immorally and experience pain and suffering, so that he can then virtuously become incarnate and atone for their moral wrongdoing? It certainly seems as if it does. But is it plausible to hold that God would play around with a created person's well-being in this way for the sake of creating a world with the great goods of incarnation and atonement?

In answer to the Munchausen-Syndrome-by-Proxy objection, Plantinga maintains that a necessary condition of God's justification for allowing evil is that the final condition of created persons be a good one, though that final good is not part of the justification for His allowing evil. Though not part of this justification, it is the case that the final condition of created persons in a world that includes the goods of incarnation and atonement "is better than it is in the worlds in which there is no fall into sin but also no incarnation and redemption" (Plantinga 2004, 25). The idea seems to be that God is not morally blameworthy for creating persons for the purpose that the goods of incarnation and atonement be instantiated, so long as the stated necessary condition of His so doing (that the final condition of created persons is a good one) is fulfilled.

What might one say about Plantinga's theodicy? Early on in his argument, he asks "[W]hat are good-making qualities among worlds—what sort of features will make one world better than another?" (Plantinga 2004, 6) Plantinga's first words in response are "Here one thinks ... of creaturely happiness ..." (Plantinga 2004, 6). This is a perfectly natural response. Why, however, does one think of this? Though Plantinga does not answer this question, he does state that "Suffering is an intrinsically bad thing" (Plantinga 2004, 15). If it is, it only stands to reason that happiness is an intrinsically good thing, and because God knows that it is and He is perfectly good and loving, He creates persons for the purpose that they experience this great good. Thus, as Plantinga says, while "we can imagine or in some sense conceive of worlds in which the only things that exist are persons always in excruciating pain" (Plantinga 2004, 6), no such world is possible "if God, as we are assuming, is a necessary being who has essentially such properties as unlimited goodness ..." (Plantinga 2004, 6).

Given that God, because of His essential properties, cannot create conceivable worlds in which creatures are always in excruciating pain, and given that it is natural to think of creaturely happiness when one thinks of good-making features of a world, it is no surprise that any world with incarnation and atonement will include at least the possibility of the experience of such a good condition by created persons. Plantinga claims, however, not only that a world with incarnation and atonement will include a final good condition for created persons, but also, as was already quoted, that this condition "is better than it is in worlds in which there is no fall into sin but also no incarnation and redemption" (Plantinga 2004, 25) What justifies this claim? Intuitively, an earthly life that includes only happiness and runs seamlessly into perfect happiness in the afterlife is on the whole better than one that includes earthly pain and suffering and ends with perfect happiness in the afterlife. Plantinga is favorably disposed toward the idea that it is by suffering that we can achieve an intimacy with God ("enjoying solidarity with [Christ]" Plantinga 2004, 18) that cannot be achieved in any other way. Perhaps, then, he believes that his claim about worlds with incarnation, atonement, sin, and suffering being better in terms of their final good condition for created persons than ones without incarnation, atonement, sin, and suffering is justified by the idea that sin and suffering make possible a level of happiness that cannot be experienced without them.

If this is Plantinga's reasoning, it is less than persuasive. After all, atheists and theists alike find it quite easy to conceive of a world in which created persons have perfect happiness without the preparatory work of sin and suffering. Indeed, it is because such a world seems better than one in which created persons experience this happiness but sin and suffer that the problem of evil presents the intellectual challenge to theistic belief that it does. Moreover, if one turns to Scripture for possible insight into the problem of evil, something which Plantinga is not averse to doing, one can easily come away (as many down through the ages have) from reading the story about the garden of Eden (Genesis 1–3) with the impression that Adam and Eve had ongoing access to the tree of life (i.e. ongoing access to continued happiness with no pain and suffering), access which would not have been lost had they not eaten of the tree of the knowledge of good and evil. In short, while one can agree with Plantinga that a world with incarnation, atonement, sin, and suffering includes the possibility of a final and exceedingly great good condition for created persons, there seemingly is no reason to think that these things are a necessary means to the achievement of this exceedingly great good condition.

What about Plantinga's claim that while it is a necessary condition of a world that includes incarnation and atonement that it also include (the possibility of) a final good condition for human beings, this necessary condition is not part of God's justification for permitting evil? Earlier in this section, I stated that it was hard to see how the possibility of experiencing perfect happiness could be a necessary condition of God's justification for allowing evil, without being that justification. Has Plantinga made it easier for us to see how this is possible?

I doubt it. To see why, consider what Plantinga says about the relationship between incarnation, atonement, sin, and suffering.

> The priority [of incarnation and atonement over sin and suffering] isn't temporal, and isn't exactly logical either; it is a matter, rather, of ultimate aim as opposed to proximate aim. God's ultimate aim, here, is to create a world of a certain level of value. That aim requires that he aim to create a world in which there is incarnation and atonement—which, in turn, requires that there be sin and evil. (Plantinga 2004, 12)

According to Plantinga, God's ultimate purpose, which is that the goods of incarnation and atonement be instantiated, explains the subsidiary purpose that sin and suffering be allowed. What is also the case is that the (possible) achievement of a final good condition for created persons is a necessary condition for creating a world that includes incarnation and atonement. Why, however, is the former a necessary condition of the latter? Plantinga would have us believe that it is because God is essentially perfectly good and loving and, therefore, must provide (the possibility of) a final good existence for persons in every world that He creates. It is not because the idea of a final good existence for created persons is conceptually related to the idea of incarnation and atonement. Is it not the case, however, that just as atonement conceptually presupposes sin (and the suffering that it causes), because it by definition is salvation from that sin (and suffering), so also it conceptually presupposes the idea of a final good condition for created persons because it is by definition *a means to accomplishing that final good*? In other words, is it not the case that just as "atonement is among other things a matter of creatures being saved from the consequences of their sin" (Plantinga 2004, 12), so also atonement is first and foremost a matter of creatures being saved *for the final good end* for which they were created? The intuitively plausible answer to this question is "Yes." In the end, by according primary place to the possibility of experiencing perfect happiness as God's justification for allowing evil, we are able to provide a more adequate conceptual integration than Plantinga does of the concepts of perfect happiness, incarnation, atonement, and sin (moral evil).

Finally, to think about the problem of evil first and foremost in terms of possible worlds and their goods runs contrary to the intuition that the good about which God is most concerned is that of individual persons. The suggestion that goods like free will, incarnation, and atonement are primary in considering what might justify God's allowance of evil puts the cart before the horse. The need for any of these goods is dependent upon the existence of individuals who are made for perfect happiness. Not happiness in the sense that God tallies up the amount of happiness of one world against that of another, but happiness in the sense that a particular person is created to be perfectly happy. God first and foremost cares about individuals and thought about the problem of evil should start with the final good of those created persons as individuals.

Justice as an organic unity

According to the theodicy that I am proposing, though free will is not itself an intrinsic good that justifies God's permission of evil, it is required for that justification, which is that those who make a just-good-seeking SFC be granted the experience of perfect happiness, where this experience is their purpose for existing. Given the place of free will in this theodicy, it is important to make clear that the possibility of experiencing perfect happiness is not an end to which the evil that results from unjust-good-seeking SFCs (or any other unjust choice) is intended by God as a means. Given foreknowledge, God foresees any evil that will result from the wrong exercise by created persons of their free will. But God does not intend the occurrence of that evil. And given that God does not intend this evil there is no minimum amount of it that must occur in accordance with God's justification for allowing it. Moreover, just as there is no minimum amount of evil, so also there is no maximum amount the exceeding of which is incompatible with God's justification for permitting it. Given free will, created persons might have chosen in ways that resulted in more experiences of evil and in ways that resulted in fewer experiences of evil, and God's justification for permitting these experiences of evil would have been consistent with either alternative.

The fact that God's justification for allowing evil is consistent with the occurrence of less evil than we find in this world raises the question of why God did not guarantee the occurrence of less evil (Mackie 1955). The answer to this question is that given that created persons have free will, God could not have guaranteed the occurrence of a specific amount of evil without eliminating some or all of the exercises of that free will. But why must creatures have free will? To reiterate, it is the intrinsic good of justice that requires the provision of free will. The experience of perfect happiness is a great good and, because it is, it cannot simply be bestowed on created persons independent of considerations of justice. The existence of justice entails that the experience of perfect happiness should go only to those who deserve it. Philosopher W. D. Ross captures this point nicely when he asks us to consider the following imaginary scenarios about states of the universe:

> If we compare two imaginary states of the universe, alike in the total amounts of virtue and vice and of pleasure and pain present in the two, but in one of which the virtuous were all happy and the vicious miserable, while in the other the virtuous were miserable and the vicious happy, very few people would hesitate to say that the first was a much better state of the universe than the second. It would seem then that ... we must recognize as a[n] ... independent good, the apportionment of pleasure and pain to the virtuous and the vicious respectively. (Ross 1930, 138)

Slote shares the intuition of Ross: "But intuitively ... one wants to say that though it is not a good thing *that* someone should benefit from wrongdoing, what is bad here is precisely that a person actually *benefits* from acting viciously" (Slote 2001, 154).

Sometimes, a good way to elucidate a point that one is trying to make (in this case, the point concerns the role of justice in explaining God's allowance of evil) is to contrast it with another point of view. To this end, consider some thoughts about the problem of evil that are developed by the philosopher Marilyn Adams. As she sees the problem of evil, there are two ways in which God might justify permitting someone to experience evil.

First, God justifies evil by "balancing it off": "The balancing-off relation is arithmetical and additive: value-parts are balanced off within a larger whole if other parts of opposite value equal or outweigh them" (Adams 1999, 21). Adams says that the problem for the balancing-off relation as a justification of evil is that some people's lives include horrendous evils, where a horrendous evil is one "the participation in which constitutes prima facie reason to doubt whether the participant's life could … be a great good to him/her on the whole…. [H]orrendous evils seem prima facie, not only to balance off but to engulf any positive value in the participant's life" (Adams 1999, 26). Examples of horrendous evil include

> the rape of a woman and axing off of her arms, psycho-physical torture whose ultimate goal is the disintegration of personality, betrayal of one's deepest loyalties, child abuse of the sort described by Ivan Karamazov, child pornography, parental incest, slow death by starvation, the explosion of nuclear bombs over populated areas…. [W]hat makes horrendous evils so pernicious is their life-ruining potential, their power prima facie to degrade the individual by devouring the possibility of positive personal meaning in one swift gulp. (Adams 1999, 26–8)

According to Adams, if theists are to present an adequate answer to horrendous evils, then they must invoke a second form of justification, which she calls the "defeat" of evil. Evil is defeated in a person's life when it is integrated into the whole of that life by means of a nonadditive relation that the philosopher G. E. Moore calls an "organic unity" (Moore 1903, 27–36; I appealed to this concept in Chapter 3, when I discussed objections to my view of life's meaning). With an organic unity, not only might the whole have a different value than a part, but also a negatively (or positively or neutrally) valued part can contribute to a great overall positive (or negative) value in the whole. Thus, horrendous evils are defeated when they make a positive contribution to the overall good of a person's life. They make this contribution by being integrated into an organic unity in that individual's life, whereby that life is worth living overall. Adams claims that there are different scenarios in which horrendous evils are defeated in this way. For example, a sufferer has a vision of God in light of the horrendous evil in his or her life, and this organic relationship defeats the evil. Or, on another scenario, a sufferer identifies it with Christ's suffering, most notably his crucifixion. This event involving Christ enables the sufferer to identify with Christ's sharing in horrendous evils, which results in a positive aspect being conferred on the sufferer's own experiences of such evils. This positive aspect is a result of the organic unity in which the horrendous evils are defeated (Adams 1999, Chapter 8).

According to Adams, horrendous evils must be defeated. However, they must also be balanced off or overbalanced by the experience of perfect happiness in the afterlife (this experience actually overbalances horrendous evils), if God is to have an adequate justification for permitting them:

> If postmortem, the individual is ushered into a relation of beatific intimacy with God and comes to recognize how past participation in horrors is thus defeated, and if his/her concrete well-being is guaranteed forever afterward so that concrete ills are balanced off, then God will have been good to that individual despite participation in horrors. (Adams 1999, 168)

Finally, Adams believes that horrendous evils would forever remain defeated and, thereby, unjustified in an individual's life, if God were to allow that person to go forever without perfect happiness. Hence, for the complete defeat and balancing-off of evil, everyone must finally experience perfect happiness.

Though there is certainly much to be embraced in Adams' theodicy (e.g. the idea of an organic unity), there are also problems. Most importantly, while she is correct when she says that perfect happiness balances off (by overbalancing) horrendous evils, she undermines the organic unity that is justice with her insistence that *everyone* finally experience perfect happiness. On my theodicy, the ultimate defeat of evil is accomplished through the intrinsic good of justice, where justice is the organic unity in which those who make a just-good-seeking SFC receive the perfect happiness for which they were created, while those who never make that SFC do not experience that happiness. Thus, while an experience of pleasure is a simple intrinsic good and the intrinsic goodness of perfect happiness is a function of arithmetically adding together experiences of pleasure, justice is a complex intrinsic good whose value arises from nonadditively arranging parts together in a proper relationship. Once again, the gist of my view is provided by Ross:

> Few people would hesitate to say that a state of affairs in which A is good and happy and B bad and unhappy is better than one in which A is good and unhappy and B bad and happy.... The surplus value of the first whole arises not from the value of its elements but from the co-presence of goodness and happiness in one single person, and of badness and unhappiness in another. (Ross 1930, 72)

Now, because the freedom to make a just-good-seeking SFC entails the freedom to make an unjust-good-seeking SFC, there is no way for God to guarantee that an individual will make the former of the two choices. Hence, there is no way for God to ensure that everyone will experience perfect happiness. Were God to bestow perfect happiness upon everyone, regardless of which choice they made, then an ultimate absurdity would prevail (which is like the concept discussed in the last section of Chapter 2, where everyone ends up in the same condition, vz. dead, regardless of whether they choose to be moral or not) and evil would defeat good. So while the concept of an organic unity is important, Adams fails to incorporate it in the right way into her theodicy.

Tying together some loose ends

Up to this point in this chapter, I have treated the problem of evil as if it were exclusively an issue of morally wrong choices and the pain that results from them (what philosophers regularly refer to as "moral evil"). However, there is evil in the world that does not present itself as moral evil. For example, there are earthquakes, tornadoes, plagues, etc., that do not appear to be the result of immoral human free choices. Does the theodicy that I propose for moral evil also work for this evil, what philosophers term "natural evil"?

Though natural evils do not appear to us to be moral in nature (which is different from their appearing not to be moral in nature), perhaps they are instances of the latter. Perhaps some of them are caused by human choices, even though we are not able to discern how they are. (E.g. some people are convinced that human use of fossil fuels is producing global warming and creating the potential for—if it has not already created—natural disasters.) If they are correct, it is surely possible that human actions have led to other natural disasters. Or perhaps the choices of nonhuman beings (e.g. fallen angels) with free will and the desire for complete happiness are ultimately responsible for the occurrence of natural evils (Plantinga 1974, 58). Or, yet another alternative is that the events that produce natural evils inevitably occur just as a part of nature and what happened is that human persons lost an original ability to protect themselves from these events when the first humans sinned (chose unjustly) (van Inwagen 1988, 168–71). In this last case, what do not appear to be moral evils are not. What is clear is that we simply do not know what the ontological status of natural evils is because we do not know what their ultimate explanation is. As a skeptical theist would say, and rightly in this context, the explanation of natural evils that do not appear to be moral in nature is beyond our ken.

While the ultimate explanation of natural evils that do not appear to be moral in nature is a matter that is beyond our epistemic wherewithal, the justification for God's permitting them is not. Regardless of whether or not natural evils are ultimately moral in nature, the theodicy I have set forth maintains that their permission is justified by the possibility of our experiencing perfect happiness. This is the justification of natural evils for the same reason that it is the justification of moral evils. Because experiencing perfect happiness is a person's greatest possible good and as such decisively outweighs any evil that he or she might experience, the possibility of experiencing it is God's justification for permitting that individual to experience evil of *any* kind.

If natural evils are ultimately moral in nature, then we not only understand *what* their justification is but also *how* that justification explains their permission, because we understand how the possibility of experiencing perfect happiness requires giving created persons the free will whose unjust exercise produces moral evil. If natural evils are ultimately not moral in nature, then while we know what the justification for permitting them is, we do not presently understand (we fail to be aware of) how that justification relates to their permission. Thus, what makes natural evils different from moral evils is not that we are ignorant about what justifies God's permission of the former, whereas we know what justifies His permission of the latter, but that we are ignorant about how, if at all, that justification explains the permission of the former.

It is relevant to note that a proponent of the problem of evil might argue that if God does exist, we would now understand whether natural evils are ultimately moral or not moral in nature and, if it is the latter, how the possibility of experiencing complete happiness is related to their permission. Our ignorance regarding these matters is itself an instance of unjustified evil.

I cannot see any good reason to believe that we would now understand the matters that the proponent of the argument claims we would understand, if God exists. While it is plausible to believe that we know what God's justification for permitting our experience of evil is, given that knowledge about these matters is not required for knowledge of this justification, our ignorance about these issues is not surprising. As skeptical theists are wont to point out, if theism is true, one would expect that God's knowledge would dwarf that of created persons. Ignorance about many things like primordial history is part and parcel of being a created person.

The experience of evil by beasts

I close this chapter with some brief thoughts about the problem of evil as it relates to beasts (nonhuman animals), many of whom seem to experience pain. What is God's justification for allowing evil into their subjective world? With regard to this issue, I believe it is reasonable for a theist to be skeptical and answer this question with "I don't know," because the matter is one that is beyond our ken. To explain why it is beyond our ken, consider once again the problem of evil as it relates to created persons. In general terms, the theodicy that I have proposed and defended maintains that knowledge of God's justification for permitting a person to experience evil presupposes knowledge of an individual's purpose for existing, where knowledge of this purpose requires awareness of a person's human nature and what is intrinsically good. Given our knowledge that a person is an entity whose nature includes free will and a desire for perfect happiness, where this happiness is intrinsically good, it is possible to know what God's justification for permitting created persons to experience evil is. When it comes to beasts, however, we lack knowledge of their purpose for existing because we lack adequate knowledge of their natures. We simply do not know enough about their psychological makeup and what the structure of their will is like, provided that they have a psychological makeup and will. As Eleonore Stump says (in my opinion, too optimistically), "everything depends on the nature of the sentience of the creature suffering; and, for very many sentient creatures, we are only beginning to understand anything about their sentience" (Stump 2010, 379).

It is important to stress at this point that being a skeptical theist with regard to the sufferings of beasts does not require that one deny that they experience pain. As Michael Murray and Glenn Ross suggest, a skeptical theist might embrace the following principle (I will dub it "SA") concerning the sufferings of animals:

> SA: Some non-human creatures have states that have intrinsic phenomenal qualities analogous to those possessed by humans when they are in states of pain. These creatures lack, however, any higher order states of being aware of themselves as being in first-order states. They have no access to the fact that they are having a particular feeling, though they are indeed having it. Since phenomenal properties of states of pain and other sensory states are intrinsic to the states themselves, there is no difference on this score between humans and other creatures. (Murray and Ross 2006, 176)

As Murray and Ross note, one might object to SA by arguing that certain experiences are bad, even where the subjects of those experiences do not possess the relevant higher order states of awareness of themselves as being in those first-order states. "Access to these states, the critic might contend, is irrelevant to whether it is bad to be in the state itself. Clearly, if a state is intrinsically bad, it is not made better merely in virtue of the fact that the creature does not know about it" (Murray and Ross 2006, 176). Murray and Ross rightly respond that a defender of SA need not deny that the pain experienced by a beast is intrinsically evil. What is in dispute is whether the experience of that pain is unjustified. The truth of SA helps to make clear that an answer to the question of whether the evil experienced by beasts is justified or not is not easy to come by. If, in the case of a beast, "there is simply no victim, no subject for whom it can be said that there is a way it is like for it to be in such a state of pain" (Murray and Ross 2006, 177), then it is not obvious that the evil is unjustified.

In light of this discussion of SA, consider an example of Rowe's involving a fawn:

> Suppose in some distant forest lightning strikes a dead tree, resulting in a forest fire. In the fire a fawn is trapped, horribly burned, and lies in terrible agony for several days before death relieves its suffering. So far as we can see, the fawn's intense suffering is pointless. For there does not appear to be any greater good such that the prevention of the fawn's suffering would require either the loss of that good or the occurrence of an evil equally bad or worse. (Rowe 1990, 129–30)

How can Rowe reasonably conclude that we are justified in believing that the fawn's suffering is pointless (and, therefore, not justifiably allowable by God, were He to exist) on the grounds that we cannot see what the point of its suffering is? Does any one of us have adequate knowledge of a fawn's psychology? Does any one of us know whether a fawn is self-aware and in possession of a concept of itself as a persisting entity that remains self-identical through time? Does any one of us know that a fawn desires the experience of perfect happiness for itself like a person desires this experience for himself or herself? Does a fawn's existence end with its death or does it have an afterlife?

If we are honest, I think that while we might believe some things about a beast's psychology (e.g. that the fawn does not have a concept of itself as a persisting, self-identical entity that desires perfect happiness for itself), we must admit that none of us knows the answers to these questions. If we do not know the answers to these questions, how is the claim that the fawn's suffering is unjustified warranted? Is it not the case that the fawn's suffering as such neither appears justified nor unjustified because we simply do not know what a fawn's nature and purpose for existing are? Is it not the case that it seems as if the fawn suffers, and the issue of whether its suffering is justified or unjustified is beyond our ken? I conclude that with regard to the suffering of beasts, it is reasonable to be a skeptical theist.

Addendum

In the section of this chapter entitled "Life Plans and Perfect Happiness," I once again had reason to mention Robert Nozick's experience machine. Variations on Nozick's experience machine abound in the literature on the meaning of life. For example, Richard Kraut describes and reacts to the following Nozick-like scenario:

> A high induced by a drug might be one of the most intense pleasures a human being can experience. Suppose it were possible to administer such a drug to a human being soon after her birth, and to keep that child alive but dysfunctional in every way for the normal span of a human life. She would lie in her hospital bed, fed by a tube through which drugs flow, and would remain in that state of truncated development for the remainder of her existence. The pleasure felt in such a life is, by hypothesis, intense, uninterrupted, certain, and long-lasting. Even so, this is not an option any sane parent would choose for a child if she could instead live a life in which her faculties grow and mature and the less intense satisfactions of a normal and happy life, albeit accompanied by some measure of disappointment, sorrow, and pain, are available to her. (Kraut 2007, 125)

I argued in this chapter that no self-conscious being deserves to experience perfect happiness, unless he or she makes the right kind of good-seeking SFC. Kraut's description of the child who is dysfunctional in every way raises serious questions about whether she ever achieves self-consciousness and is capable of making the choice that is requisite for experiencing perfect happiness. Because choices presuppose beliefs and desires about alternatives from which to choose, a self-conscious being capable of making choices must possess a substantive mental life. It seems reasonable, then, to require that a subject in a Nozick-like scenario be a person with various mental capacities, such as the capacity to be aware of objects (including him- or herself), the capacity to choose, the capacity to believe, and the capacity to desire.

Now, consider Galen Strawson's example of Weather Watchers:

> The Weather Watchers are a race of sentient, intelligent creatures. They are distributed about the surface of their planet, rooted to the ground, profoundly interested in the local weather. They

have sensations, thoughts, emotions, beliefs, desires. They possess a conception of an objective, spatial world. But they are constitutionally incapable of any sort of behavior, as this is ordinarily understood. They lack the necessary physiology. Their mental lives have no other-observable effects. They are not even disposed to behave in any way. (Strawson 1994, 251)

Let us stipulate that God is analogous to the parent in Kraut's example. Is it conceptually coherent to think that Weather Watchers, rooted to the ground and incapable of interaction with fellow Weather Watchers, could be perfectly happy because God guarantees that they receive nothing but pleasure from continually observing the weather (they receive this pleasure for having made the right good-seeking SFC in an earlier life)? I cannot see any reason to deny the conceptual coherence of such a scenario. The Weather Watchers are perfectly happy. Would God be sane in granting such an existence to the Weather Watchers? I cannot see any reason to deny sanity in this situation. Would I mind becoming a Weather Watcher? Given that I would be perfectly happy, surely not. Might perfect happiness be bestowed on God Watchers (those who are profoundly interested in God)? I cannot find any conceptual problem with such a scenario. Would I mind being a God Watcher? By no means, given that I would be perfectly happy watching God (e.g. beholding God in the beatific vision).

In short, when one strips away the nonessential elements of Nozick stories that seem designed to suggest the subject involved is not really perfectly happy (in Kraut's example, being completely dysfunctional, lying in a hospital bed, being fed through a tube), the idea that the character in such a story cannot be perfectly happy seems implausible. Moreover, notice that Kraut says that it would be better to have a life with some measure of disappointment, sorrow, and pain in it than to be the child in his example. Would he say the same thing in comparison to being a Weather Watcher? A God Watcher? If Kraut is right, what happens to the problem of evil? Is there no such problem?

At a minimum, it is reasonable to think that the experience of perfect happiness will occur in an ongoing, eternal personal relationship with God because the recipient of perfect happiness will desire to be able to continue expressing gratitude for his or her experience of perfect happiness. Moreover, as I emphasized in

Chapter 3, I see no reason to deny that perfect happiness in the afterlife will include bodily activity in a community of believers who share that desire. I affirm the bodily nature of this community as an adherent of Christian theism, which maintains that there will be a bodily existence (the resurrection of the body) and activity in the life everlasting. I do not say this on philosophical grounds, which, except for considerations of justice, leave wide open the means God might use to bring it about that we experience nothing but pleasure. I suspect that when philosophers such as Kraut pose their Nozick-like counterexamples and insist that we would not choose to have a loved one connected to the experience machine, they are thinking more about themselves than their loved one. The reason why they would not make such a choice is that they would no longer be able to derive pleasure from interactions with that person.

In the end, the experience machine, absent considerations of justice, not only drives home the point that happiness is something we can experience without doing anything, but also makes clear that its association with certain actions and not others is a fact about which we ultimately have no say and are, once again, thoroughly passive. The conjunction of happiness with actions of various kinds is something we discover and do not decide. It is arranged for us. And the fact that there is an arrangement at all is something at which to marvel and for which to be thankful.

6

Conclusion

In Chapter 1, I posed the following three questions about the meaning of life:

1 What is the meaning of life?
2 What makes life meaningful?
3 Is life meaningful?

Given the treatment of a veritable host of issues in the preceding five chapters, it is appropriate to conclude by reconsidering these three questions.

Question (1) is plausibly understood as asking "What is the purpose of life?" According to the theistic account that I have set forth in this book, God has created individual human persons for the purpose that each experience perfect happiness. In providing this answer to the question, I have not in the least considered myself to be developing a novel idea. To the contrary, I have taken myself to be stating the obvious. Given the obvious nature of my answer, I have not really tried to argue for it beyond defending it against criticisms, for how can one make what is obvious more believable than it already is? But a defense of what is obvious about the purpose of life is certainly needed, because so many, including both atheists and theists, seem either to have somehow missed it or to have knowingly covered it up.

Question (2) is reasonably construed as asking "What makes life worth living?" The answer is related to that given to question (1): happiness is what makes life worth living and thus it is the purpose for which God creates a human person. Moreover, I have affirmed that happiness is identical with (in the sense that it consists of) experiences of pleasure absent any experiences of pain. I have also taken this identification of happiness with experiences of pleasure without any experiences of pain to be something that is obvious. The assertion of this identity, like the affirmation that life's purpose is to experience perfect happiness, is in no way novel (what is obvious cannot be novel), though it is currently controversial and vigorously contested. Given its contentiousness, I spent a good bit of time and space defending it in Chapters 2 and 3. The only thing that I would stress at this juncture is that I have in no way misled the reader as to the scope and depth of the opposition in recent decades among many philosophers and some scientists to the view that what makes life worth living is a matter of what we experience. Indeed, these philosophers and scientists have made a concerted effort to develop views of life that marginalize, if not totally eliminate, the reality and importance of what we (consciously) experience in human life. One of the central figures in this ongoing assault, the philosopher Jaegwon Kim, has penned the following description of the contemporary scene:

> For most of us, there is no need to belabor the centrality of consciousness to our conception of ourselves as creatures with minds. But I want to point to the ambivalent, almost paradoxical, attitude that philosophers [e.g., naturalists; see Chapter 4] have displayed toward consciousness.... [C]onsciousness had been virtually banished from the philosophical and scientific scene for much of the last century, and consciousness-bashing still goes on in some quarters, with some reputable philosophers arguing that phenomenal consciousness, or "qualia," is a fiction of bad philosophy. And there are philosophers ... who, while they recognize phenomenal consciousness as something real do not believe that a complete science of human behavior, including cognitive psychology and neuroscience, has a place for consciousness in an explanatory/predictive theory of cognition and behavior....
>
> Contrast this lowly status of consciousness in science and metaphysics with its lofty standing in moral philosophy and value theory. When philosophers discuss the nature of the intrinsic good, or what is worthy of our desire and volition for its own sake, the most prominently mentioned candidates are things like pleasure, absence of pain, enjoyment, and happiness .... To most of us, a fulfilling life, a life worth living, is one that

is rich and full in qualitative consciousness. We would regard life as impoverished and not fully satisfying if it never included experiences of things like the smell of the sea in a cool morning breeze, the lambent play of sunlight on brilliant autumn foliage, the fragrance of a field of lavender in bloom, and the vibrant, layered soundscape projected by a string quartet.... It is an ironic fact that the felt qualities of conscious experience, perhaps the only things that ultimately matter to us, are often relegated in the rest of philosophy to the status of "secondary qualities," in the shadowy zone between the real and the unreal, or even jettisoned outright as artifacts of confused minds. (Kim 2005, pp. 10–12)

If I am right, no view of what makes life worth living that marginalizes consciousness in general and experiences of pleasure and pain in particular can even come close to being right. This is the case because experiences of pleasure and pain are the primary loci of positive and negative value, respectively: pleasure is intrinsically good and pain is intrinsically evil, and it is because they are so that they are at the heart of what makes life worth living and we care so deeply about them.

The values possessed by pleasure and pain are nonmoral in nature and their primacy entails that moral value is secondary in nature. Thus, certain actions are moral/just and others immoral/unjust only because of the values possessed by pleasure and pain. While moral value is secondary, it is nevertheless at the forefront of our minds when it comes to choosing how to live life. We desire to experience pleasure, but on many occasions are informed by others and ultimately our own consciences not to pursue it in this or that way. "Restrain yourself" is the admonition. And this takes us to question (3) about the meaning of life, which is "Is life meaningful?" This question is most plausibly understood to be asking "Does life make any sense in terms of things fitting together in an intelligible way?" In the present context, this means "Does it make sense for a person to sacrifice his or her opportunity to experience pleasure through material goods for the purpose of acting morally?" I argued at length in Chapter 2 that restraint of this kind makes sense and is ultimately justifiable only if death is not our final end and God exists to make sure that happiness and morality meet and embrace in the afterlife. If they do embrace, then things fit together as they should in the end because the desire for perfect happiness is fulfilled.

However, theism bears its own distinctive burden concerning the question of whether life makes any sense in terms of things fitting together in an intelligible way in the form of the problem of evil, which is the question of why evil exists if God knows all that can be known, is all-powerful, and is perfectly good (which is manifested in His creating us for perfect happiness). I argued in Chapter 5 that our knowledge that perfect happiness is the purpose of life is of central importance in providing an answer to the problem of evil. For too long now, theists have sought to address this problem in terms of possible worlds that God might create and their values. This strikes me as simply wrongheaded. God is first and foremost concerned with individual persons and their good, not with the good of a world. And the good of persons is their happiness, which consists of pleasure.

BIBLIOGRAPHY

Adams, Marilyn McCord. 1999. *Horrendous Evils and the Goodness of God*. Ithaca: Cornell University Press.

Alston, William P. 1996a. "Some (Temporarily) Final Thoughts on Evidential Arguments from Evil." In Daniel Howard-Snyder (ed.), *The Evidential Argument from Evil*. Bloomington: Indiana University Press, pp. 311–32.

—. 1996b. "The Inductive Argument from Evil and the Human Cognitive Condition." In Daniel Howard-Snyder (ed.), *The Evidential Argument from Evil*. Bloomington: Indiana University Press, pp. 97–125.

—. 2002. "What Euthyphro Should Have Said." In William Lane Craig (ed.), *Philosophy of Religion: A Reader and Guide*. New Brunswick, NJ: Rutgers University Press, pp. 283–98.

Armstrong, David. 1978. "Naturalism, Materialism, and First Philosophy." *Philosophia* 8: 261–76.

—. 1999. *The Mind-Body Problem: An Opinionated Introduction*. Boulder, CO: Westview Press.

Augustine, St. 1961. *Confessions*. Translated by R. S. Pine-Coffin. New York: Penguin Books.

—. 1993. *The City of God*. Translated by Micheal Dods. New York: The Modern Library.

Bagger, Matthew. 1999. *Religious Experience, Justification, and History*. Cambridge: Cambridge University Press.

Baggett, David and Jerry L. Walls. 2011. *Good God: The Theistic Foundations of Morality*. New York: Oxford University Press.

Baggini, Julian. 2004. *What's It All About? Philosophy and the Meaning of Life*. New York: Oxford University Press.

Baier, Kurt. 2000. "The Meaning of Life." In Elmer Daniel Klemke (ed.), *The Meaning of Life*. 2nd edn. NewYork: Oxford University Press, pp. 101–32.

Baumeister, Ray F. 2010. "Understanding Free Will and Consciousness on the Basis of Current Research Findings in Psychology." In Ray F. Baumeister, Alfred R. Mele, and Kathleen D. Vohs (eds), *Free Will and Consciousness: How Might They Work?* New York: Oxford University Press, pp. 24–42.

Behe, Michael J. 1996. *Darwin's Black Box*. New York: The Free Press.
Bloom, Paul. 2004. *Descartes' Baby: How the Science of Child Development Explains What Makes Us Human*. New York: Basic Books.
Bok, Sissela. 2010. *Exploring Happiness: From Aristotle to Brain Science*. New Haven: Yale University Press.
Bratman, Michael. 1987. *Intentions, Plans, and Practical Reason*. Cambridge, MA: Harvard University Press.
Camus, Albert. 2000. "The Absurdity of Human Existence." In Elmer Daniel Klemke (ed.), *The Meaning of Life*. 2nd edn. NewYork: Oxford University Press, pp. 94–100.
Chalmers, David. 1996. *The Conscious Mind: In Search of a Fundamental Theory*. New York: Oxford University Press.
Charry, Ellen T. 2010. *God and the Art of Happiness*. Grand Rapids, MI: William B. Eerdmans Publishing Company.
Churchland, Patricia S. 2011. *Braintrust: What Neuroscience Tells Us about Morality*. Princeton: Princeton University Press.
Craig, William Lane. 2009. "The Kurtz/Craig Debate: Is Goodness without God Good Enough?" and "This Most Gruesome of Guests." In Robert K. Garcia and Nathan L. King (eds), *Is Goodness without God Good Enough? A Debate on Faith, Secularism, and Ethics*. Lanham, MD: Rowman and Littlefield, pp. 25–46, 117–31.
Crisp, Roger. 2006. *Reasons and the Good*. Oxford: Clarendon Press.
Dancy, Jonathan. 2000. *Practical Reality*. Oxford: Oxford University Press.
Darwin, Charles. 1989. *Voyage of the Beagle*. New York: Penguin.
Davidman, Joy. 2009. *Out of My Bones: The Letters of Joy Davidman*. Edited by Don W. King. Grand Rapids, MI: Eerdmans.
Dawkins, Richard. 1989. *The Selfish Gene* (new edn). New York: Oxford University Press.
Dennett, Daniel. 2003. *Freedom Evolves*. New York: Viking.
—. 2006. *Breaking the Spell: Religion as a Natural Phenomenon*. New York: Viking.
Descartes, René. 1967. *The Philosophical Works of Descartes*. Vol. 1. Translated by Elizabeth S. Haldane and George Robert Thomson Ross. Cambridge: Cambridge University Press.
Eagleton, Terry. 2007. *The Meaning of Life: A Very Short Introduction*. New York: Oxford University Press.
Edwards, Paul. 2000. "The Meaning and Value of Life." In Elmer Daniel Klemke (ed.), *The Meaning of Life*. 2nd edn. NewYork: Oxford University Press, pp. 133–52.
Feynman, Richard. 1998. *The Meaning of It All*. Reading, MA: Perseus Books.
Fischer, John Martin. 1994. "Why Immortality Is Not So Bad." *International Journal of Philosophical Studies* 2: 257–70.

—. 2009. "Free Will, Death, and Immortality: The Role of Narrative."
  In John Martin Fischer (ed.), *Our Stories: Essays on Life, Death, and
  Free Will*. New York: Oxford University Press, pp. 145–64.
Flanagan, Owen. 2000. "What Makes Life Worth Living." In Elmer
  Daniel Klemke (ed.), *The Meaning of Life*. 2nd edn. New York: Oxford
  University Press, pp. 198–206.
—. 2002. *The Problem of the Soul*. New York: Basic Books.
—. 2009. *The Really Hard Problem: Meaning in a Material World*.
  Cambridge, MA: MIT Press.
Futuyma, Douglas. 1982. *Science on Trial: The Case for Evolution*.
  New York: Pantheon Books.
Geach, Peter. 1956. "Good and Evil." *Analysis*, 17: 32–42.
Goetz, Stewart. 2005. "Substance Dualism." In Joel B. Green and Stuart
  L. Palmer (eds), *In Search of the Soul*. Downers Grove, IL: InterVarsity
  Press, pp. 33–60.
Goetz, Stewart and Charles Taliaferro. 2011. *A Brief History of the Soul*.
  United Kingdom: Wiley-Blackwell.
Goetz, Stewart and Mark Baker. 2011. *The Soul Hypothesis*. New York:
  Continuum.
Gordon, Jeffrey. 1984. "Is the Existence of God Relevant to the Meaning
  of Life?" *The Modern Schoolman* 60: 227–46.
Harris, Sam. 2010. *The Moral Landscape: How Science Can Determine
  Human Values*. New York: Free Press.
Haybron, Daniel. 2008. *The Pursuit of Unhappiness: The Elusive
  Psychology of Well-Being*. New York: Oxford University Press.
Hume, David. 1963. *The Philosophy of David Hume*. Edited by
  V. C. Chappell. New York: The Modern Library.
Kane, Robert. 1996. *The Significance of Free Will*. Oxford: Oxford
  University Press.
Kant, Immanuel. 1963. *Lectures on Ethics*. Translated by Louis Infield.
  New York: Harper Torchbooks.
Kekes, John. 2008. "The Meaning of Life." In Elmer Daniel Klemke
  and Steven M. Cahn (eds), *The Meaning of Life*. 3rd edn. New York:
  Oxford University Press, pp. 239–58.
Kim, Jaegwon. 1996. *Philosophy of Mind*. Boulder, CO: Westview.
—. 2005. *Physicalism, or Something Near Enough*. Princeton: Princeton
  University Press.
Krauss, Lawrence M. 2009. "God and Science Don't Mix."
  Wall Street Journal, June 26. http://online.wsj.com/article/
  SB124597314928257169.html
Kraut, Richard. 2007. *What Is Good and Why: The Ethics of Well-Being*.
  Cambridge, MA: Harvard University Press.
Kronen, John and Eric Reitan. 2011. *God's Final Victory: A Comparative
  Philosophical Case for Universalism*. New York: Continuum Press.

Kronman, Anthony T. 2007. *Education's End: Why Our Colleges and Universities Have Given Up on the Meaning of Life*. New Haven: Yale University Press

Lewis, Clive Staples. 1942. *A Preface to Paradise Lost*. New York: Oxford University Press.

—. 1961. *The Screwtape Letters*. New York: Macmillan.

—. 1962. *The Problem of Pain*. New York: Macmillan.

—. 1967. *Christian Reflections*. Grand Rapids, MI: Eerdmans.

—. 1970. *God in the Dock*. Grand Rapids, MI: Eerdmans.

—. 1984. *The Last Battle*. New York: Harper Collins.

—. 1986. *Reflections on the Psalms*. New York: Harcourt.

—. 1988. The Four Loves. New York: Harcourt

—. 1992. *Letters to Malcolm: Chiefly on Prayer*. New York: Harcourt.

—. 2001a. *Mere Christianity*. New York: Harper San Francisco.

—. 2001b. *The Great Divorce*. New York: Harper San Francisco.

—. 2004. *The Collected Letters of C. S. Lewis: Books, Broadcasts, and The War 1931–49*. Edited by Walter Hooper. New York: Harper San Francisco.

Linville, Mark. "Moral Particularism." In R. Keith Loftin (ed.), *God and Morality: Four Views*. Downers Grove, IL: InterVarsity Press. Forthcoming.

McGinn, Colin. 1991. *The Problem of Consciousness*. Oxford: Blackwell.

MacIntyre, Alasdair. 1981. *After Virtue*. Notre Dame, IN: University of Notre Dame Press

Mackie, John. 1955. "Evil and Omnipotence." *Mind* 64: 200–12.

McMahon, Darrin M. 2006. *Happiness: A History*. New York: Atlantic Monthly Press.

Matthews, Gareth B. 2005. *Augustine*. Oxford: Blackwell.

Mavrodes, George. 1986. "Religion and the Queerness of Morality." In Robert Audi and William J. Wainwright (eds), *Rationality, Religious Belief, and Moral Commitment*. Ithaca: Cornell University Press, pp. 213–26.

Melnyk, Andrew. 2007. "A Case for Physicalism about the Human Mind." Available at http://www.infidels.org/library/modern/andrew_melnyk/physicalism.html.

Midgley, Mary. 2010. *The Solitary Self: Darwin and the Selfish Gene*. Durham: Acumen.

Mill, John Stuart. 1979. *Utilitarianism*. Indianapolis, IN: Hackett.

Moore, George Edward. 1903. *Principia Ethica*. Cambridge: Cambridge University Press.

Mother Teresa. 2007. *Come Be My Light: The Private Writings of the 'Saint of Calcutta'*. Edited by Brian Kolodiejchuk, M. C. New York: Doubleday.

Mouw, Richard J. 1990. *The God Who Commands*. Notre Dame, IN: University of Notre Dame Press.

Murphy, Mark C. 2009. "Theism, Atheism, and the Explanation of Moral Value." In Robert K. Garcia and Nathan L. King (eds), *Is Goodness without God Good Enough? A Debate on Faith, Secularism, and Ethics*. Lanham, MD: Rowman and Littlefield, pp. 117–31.

Murray, Michael J. and Glenn Ross. 2006. "Neo-Cartesianism and the Problem of Animal Suffering." *Faith and Philosophy* 23: 169–90.

Nagel, Thomas. 1979. *Mortal Questions*. Cambridge: Cambridge University Press.

—. 1986. *The View from Nowhere*. New York: Oxford University Press.

—. 1997. *The Last Word*. New York: Oxford University Press.

—. 2000. "The Absurd." In Elmer Daniel Klemke (ed.), *The Meaning of Life*. 2nd edn. New York: Oxford University Press, pp. 176–85.

—. 2010. *Secular Philosophy and the Religious Temperament: Essays 2002–8*. New York: Oxford University Press.

Nielsen, Kai. 2000. "Death and the Meaning of Life." In Elmer Daniel Klemke (ed.), *The Meaning of Life*. 2nd edn. NewYork: Oxford University Press, pp. 153–9.

Nozick, Robert. 1974. *Anarchy, State, and Utopia*. New York: Basic Books.

—. 1981. *Philosophical Explorations*. Cambridge, MA: The Belknap Press.

Papineau, David. 1993. *Philosophical Naturalism*. Oxford: Blackwell.

—. 2002. *Thinking about Consciousness*. Oxford: Oxford University Press.

Penfield, Wilder. 1975. *The Mystery of the Mind*. Princeton: Princeton University Press.

Piper, John. 2011. *Desiring God: Meditations of a Christian Hedonist*. (revised edn). Colorado Springs, CO: Multnomah Books.

Plantinga, Alvin. 1974. *God, Freedom and Evil*. Grand Rapids, MI: Eerdmans.

—. 1996. "Epistemic Probability and Evil." In Daniel Howard-Snyder (ed.), *The Evidential Argument from Evil*. Bloomington: Indiana University Press, pp. 69–96.

—. 2004. "Supralapsarianism, or 'O Felix Culpa.'" In Peter van Inwagen (ed.), *Christian Faith and the Problem of Evil*. Grand Rapids, MI: Eerdmans, pp. 1–25.

Plato. 1961. *Plato: Collected Dialogues*. Edited by Edith Hamilton and Huntington Cairns. Princeton: Princeton University Press.

—. 1998a. *Four Texts on Socrates: Plato's Euthyphro, Apology, and Crito and Aristophanes' Clouds*. Translated by Thomas G. and Grace Starry West. Ithaca: Cornell University Press.

—. 1998b. *Phaedo*. Translated by Eva Brann, Peter Kalkavage, and Eric Salem. Newburyport, MA: Focus Classical Library.

Polman, Dick. 1989. "Telling the Truth, Paying the Price." *Philadelphia Inquirer Magazine*, June 18, 16–21, 26–34.

Pope Benedict XVI. 2011. Epiphany Mass, St. Peter's Basilica. January 6. http://www.msnbc.msn.com/id/40945242/ns/technology_and_science-science/t/god-was- behind-big-bang-pope-says/.

Rorty, Richard. 1979. *Philosophy and the Mirror of Nature*. Princeton: Princeton University Press.

Rosenberg, Alex. 2011a. *The Atheist's Guide to Reality: Enjoying Life without Illusions*. New York: W. W. Norton & Company.

—. 2011b. "Why I Am a Naturalist." http://opinionator.blogs.nytimes. com/2011/09/17why-i-am-a-naturalist/.

Ross, William David. 1930. *The Right and the Good*. Oxford: Clarendon Press.

Rowe, William. 1986. "The Empirical Argument from Evil." In Robert Audi and William J. Wainwright (eds), *Rationality, Religious Belief, and Moral Commitment*. Ithaca: Cornell University Press, pp. 227–47.

—. 1990. "The Problem of Evil and Some Varieties of Atheism." In Marilyn McCord and Robert Merrihew Adams (eds), *The Problem of Evil*. Oxford: Oxford University Press, pp. 126–37.

Ruse, Michael. 1998. *Taking Darwin Seriously*. Amherst, NY: Prometheus Books.

Russell, Bertrand. 2000. "A Free Man's Worship." In Elmer Daniel Klemke (ed.), *The Meaning of Life*. 2nd edn. New York: Oxford University Press, pp. 71–7.

Sartre, Jean-Paul. 1995. "There Is No Human Nature." In Gail M. Presby, Karsten J. Struhl, and Richard E. Olsen (eds), *The Philosophical Quest: A Cross-Cultural Reader*. New York: McGraw-Hill, Inc., pp. 213–21.

Seachris, Joshua. 2009. "The Meaning of Life as Narrative: A New Proposal for Interpreting Philosophy's 'Primary' Question." *Philo* 12: 5–23.

—. 2011. "Death, Futility, and the Proleptic Power of Narrative Ending." *Religious Studies* 47: 141–63.

Searle, John. 1983. *Intentionality*. Cambridge: Cambridge University Press.

Shermer, Michael. 2011. "The Enduring Appeal of the Apocalypse." *Wall Street Journal*, May 14–15, C3.

Sinnott-Armstrong, Walter. 2009. *Morality without God?* New York: Oxford University Press.

Slote, Michael. 1983. *Goods and Virtues*. Oxford: Clarendon Press.

—. 2001. *Morals from Motives*. Oxford: Oxford University Press.

Stace, Walter. 2000. "Man against Darkness." In Elmer Daniel Klemke (ed.), *The Meaning of Life*. 2nd edn. New York: Oxford University Press, pp. 84–93.

Strawson, Galen. 1994. *Mental Reality*. Cambridge, MA: MIT Press.

Stroud, Barry. 2004. "The Charm of Naturalism." In Mario de Caro and David Macarthur (eds), *Naturalism in Question*. Cambridge, MA: Harvard University Press, pp. 21–35.

Stump, Eleonore. 2010. *Wandering in Darkness: Narratives and the Problem of Suffering*. Oxford: Clarendon Press.

Talbott, Thomas. 2001. "Freedom, Damnation, and the Power to Sin with Impunity." *Religious Studies* 37: 417–34.

Taliaferro, Charles. 1994. *Consciousness and the Mind of God*. Cambridge: Cambridge University Press.

—. 2009. "Jesus Christ and the Meaning of Life." In Paul K. Moser (ed.), *Jesus and Philosophy: New Essays*. Cambridge: Cambridge University Press.

Taylor, Richard. 1992. *Metaphysics* (4th edn). Englewood Cliffs, NJ: Prentice-Hall.

—. 2000. "The Meaning of Life." In Elmer Daniel Klemke (ed.), *The Meaning of Life*. 2nd edn. New York: Oxford University Press, pp. 167–75.

Thagard, Paul. 2010. *The Brain and the Meaning of Life*. Princeton: Princeton University Press.

Van Inwagen, Peter. 1988. "The Magnitude, Duration, and Distribution of Evil: A Theodicy." *Philosophical Topics* 16: 161–88.

Walls, Jerry. 2002. *Heaven: The Logic of Eternal Joy*. New York: Oxford University Press.

Ward, Keith. 1998. *In Defense of the Soul*. Oxford: Oneworld Publishing Ltd.

Ward, Michael. 2008. *Planet Narnia*. New York: Oxford University Press.

Wegner, Daniel M. 2002. *The Illusion of Conscious Will*. Cambridge, MA: MIT Press.

Wielenberg, Erik J. 2005. *Values and Virtues in a Godless Universe*. Cambridge: Cambridge University Press.

Williams, Bernard. 1973. "The Makropulos Case: Reflections on the Tedium of Immortality." In Bernard Williams (ed.), *Problems of the Self*. Cambridge: Cambridge University Press, pp. 82–100.

Wilson, David Sloan. 2002. *Darwin's Cathedral: Evolution, Religion, and the Nature of Society*. Chicago: University of Chicago Press.

INDEX

passion (passivity, patient) 12–15,
    34–5, 85–7, 106–7, 147, 174
Paul, St 50, 71, 83, 145
Penfield, Wilder 120–2
perfection 14
Piper, John 74
Plantinga, Alvin 138, 155, 157,
    159–63, 168
Plato 18, 25–6, 98–100
pleasure 9–16, 18–19, 31–4, 36–8,
    54, 59, 65, 73–94, 127–33,
    140, 175–7
Polman, Dick 52
problem of evil 42–4, 137–74
propositional attitudes 100–3
purpose in life versus of life 44–6,
    100, 109–10, 137–40, 169

quantum indeterminacy 97–8,
    123–4

reason and religion xi, 2, 137
Reck, Erich 39
Reitan, Eric 52, 87
Rorty, Richard 113
Rosenberg, Alex 95, 113
Ross, Glenn 170–1
Ross, W. D. 164, 167
Rowe, William 156–7, 171
Ruse, Michael 57, 59
Russell, Bertrand 48–50, 59

Sarte, Jean-Paul 4, 7, 14–16, 96, 100
science 109–10, 115, 120–6
Seachris, Joshua 152–3
Searle, John 102
self-forming choice 141–6,
    149–50, 153–4, 166–7

Shermer, Michael 41
Sinnott-Armstrong, William 60–3
Sisyphus 3–4, 12–13, 86
skeptical theism 138, 154–9,
    168–9, 171
Slote, Michael 151–2, 164
Socrates 18, 25, 98–100, 120
soul 23–6, 35, 91, 114–15,
    117–18, 121, 123–4, 133
Stace, Walter 49, 126–7
Strawson, Galen 172–3
Stroud, Barry 95
Stump, Eleonore 170

Talbott, Thomas 40
Taliaferro, Charles 24, 88, 112
Taylor, Richard 3–4, 7, 12,
    15–16, 86, 115–17
Teresa, Mother 31–2, 53
Thagard, Paul 34–5

van Inwagen, Peter 168
virtue 86–8

Walls, Jerry 40, 76
Ward, Keith 75–6
Ward, Michael 92–3
Wegner, Daniel 102
well-being (best interest, prudential
    value) 15, 17–18, 32,
    49–50, 53–6, 60–9, 75,
    80–2, 87, 90–1, 140, 150,
    156, 160
Westminster shorter catechism 74
Wielenberg, Erik 69–70
Williams, Bernard 35, 38, 107
Wilson, David Sloan 129

Thank God you have that arrow.

→ RefiLL GoAL

LoL   GoALS?

depArtcol

9 781441 180827